PROFESSIONAL ISSUES FOR TRANSLATORS AND INTERPRETERS

The American Translators Association *Series* is a hardcover monograph published periodically by Johns Benjamin Publishing Company through the auspices of the Center for Research in Translation, Binghamton University. Since contributions are solicited by the Editors, prospective contributors are urged to query the Managing Editor or Theme Editor before submission. The themes and editors for Volumes VIII and IX are as follows: *Translation and the Law*, Marshall Morris, editor, University of Rio Piedras (Pelegrina 996, Santa Rita, Río Piedras, Puerto Rico 00925); *World Languages vis-à-vis Linguistic Nationalism*, Marian Labrum, Brigham Young University (Spanish and Portuguese, Brigham Young University, Provo, Utah 84602).

Back volumes of the ATA *Series* may be ordered from John Benjamins Publishing Company Amsterdam (P.O. Box 75577, 1070 An Amsterdam, The Netherlands) or Philadelphia (821 Bethlehem Pike, Philadelphia, PA 19118, USA). Volumes I (*Translation Excellence*, edited by Marilyn Gaddis Rose) and III (*Translation and Interpreter Training and Foreign Language Pedagogy*, edited by Peter W. Krawutschke) are out of print. Available volumes are as follows:

Volume II *Technology as Translation Strategy*. Guest editor: Muriel Vasconcellos, Washington, D.C.

Volume IV *Interpreting–Yesterday, Today, and Tomorrow*. Guest editors: David and Margareta Bowen, Georgetown University.

Volume V *Translation: Theory and Practice. Tension and Interdependence*. Guest editor: Mildred L. Larson, Summer Institute of Linguistics (Dallas, Texas).

Volume VI *Scientific and Technical Translation*. Guest editors: Sue Ellen and Leland D. Wright, Jr., Kent State University

Managing Editor: Marilyn Gaddis Rose, Center for Research in Translation, Binghamton University, P.O. Box 6000, Binghamton, New York, 13902-6000 USA. Editorial Advisory Board: Deanna L. Hammond, Library of Congress (Washington, D.C.); Peter W. Krawutschke, Western Michigan University (Kalamazoo); Marian Labrum, Brigham Young University (Provo, Utah); Marshall Morris, University of Puerto Rico-Rio Piedras; and Sue Ellen Wright, Institute for Applied Linguistics, Kent State University (Kent, Ohio).

Professional Issues for Translators and Interpreters

AMERICAN TRANSLATORS ASSOCIATION
SCHOLARLY MONOGRAPH *Series*

Volume VII 1994

EDITED BY

Deanna L. Hammond

JOHN BENJAMINS PUBLISHING COMPANY
AMSTERDAM/PHILADELPHIA

Library of Congress Cataloging Serial Number 87-658269

© Binghamton University, 1994
John Benjamins Publishing Company, Amsterdam/Philadelphia
ISSN 0890-4111 / ISBN 90 272 3182 6 (Eur) / 1-55619-626-1 (USA)

All Rights reserved. No part of this publication may be reproduced or transmitted in any form or by any means without prior written permission from the Publisher.

Printed in The Netherlands

American Translators Association *Series*

PROFESSIONAL ISSUES
FOR TRANSLATORS AND INTERPRETERS

Volume VII   1994

Contents

Editor's Remarks DEANNA L. HAMMOND	1
Section 1. Achieving Success as a Language Professional	
The Paradox of Professionalism NANCY SNYDER	13
The Value of Local Translator Groups ANN C. SHERWIN	23

Getting It in Writing: The Key to Problem-Free Business
    Relationships
    JANE MAIER
	35

Section 2. Challenges in a Global Economy

World Events Create Opportunies and Challenges for　　47
    Translators and Interpreters: Translating Words
    Is But a Part
    HELEN M. AND JOHN F. SZABLYA
Translation and International Trade　　59
    DORIS GANSER

Section 3. Ethics and the Profession

Professional Ethics for Court and Community Interpreters　　79
    NANCY SCHWEDA NICHOLSON
Ethics for Translators and Translation Businesses　　99
    GABE BOKOR

Section 4. Challenges of Technology

The Issues of Machine Translation　　109
    MURIEL VASCONCELLOS
The Translator Workstation　　127
    ALAN K. MELBY

Section 5. Current Economic and Legal Issues

Translation and Interpreting in the 90s:　　151
    Major Economic and Legal Issues Confronting
    the Community
    BERNARD BIERMAN

Section 6. Translator/Interpreter Training in the U.S.

The Role of the University in the Professionalization　　171
    of the Translator
    ANNE CORDERO
Ingredients to Success as a Language Specialist　　181
    MARGARETA BOWEN

Non-Discriminatory Approaches in Translation Studies DAVID BOWEN	193
The Current Status of U.S. Translator and Interpreter Training WILLIAM M. PARK	201
Contributors	206
ATA Corporate/Institutional Members	208
ATA Officers and Board of Directors, 1994	215
ATA Gode Medal Winners	215

Editor's Remarks

The title of this book, *Professional Issues in Translation and Interpretation,* is based on the premise that translating and interpreting are professions. Although not all those who render translations or engage in interpreting are professionals—in fact, a significant number of them are not—it is the premise of the authors of this volume that the profession is real and that it is growing.

Identifying all of the issues of concern to professionals in translation and interpreting would have been difficult, just as it would have been to find writers willing to contribute articles on all of the topics perceived as issues. Therefore, this guest editor makes no claims as to the completeness of the volume. Rather, it represents a collection of articles on many of the issues about which the contributors can speak with some authority. The purpose of these introductory remarks is both to reinforce some of the observations made by the contributors and to touch on some issues not treated elsewhere in this volume.

Educating the Public and the Client

An on-going issue in the profession is how to educate the public and the clients. This is usually of interest whether a translator is a freelance, an in-house translator, a professor of translation, a bureau owner, or a part-time translator. In the minds of Joe Q. Public, translator equals interpreter. Many of us, when telling someone we are a translator, have heard on more than one occasion, "Oh, a translator! And how many languages do you speak?" And few of us have failed to notice the "Voice of the Translator" on the television screen while an interpreter is talking.

Nor does the public at large, not to mention clients at times, appreciate all of the skills needed in order to become a competent translator. Many of us have heard a requester say, "I'd do it myself, but I don't have the time," or "It shouldn't take you long. It's quite simple," when actually it isn't. Many believe that with the help of a good dictionary, virtually anyone with a little language background could do the translation in question. Then there are the clients who think that a translation can be rendered more quickly than the translator can even type. Furthermore, those of us in supervisory positions are also all-too-familiar with the onslaught of recent graduates in foreign languages who come to our offices or inundate us with job applications because they do not want to be teachers so decide that for some reason it would be fun to be a translator. Such concerns as these may be addressed by individuals or by professional associations. As Sherwin, Ganser and the Szablyas note in their essays in this volume, however, individuals should not rely on others to do all the public relations: they too have a role to play.

The need for education also applies to many parts of the government. For a number of years now, individuals and language associations have been concerned about how to get more government recognition of the profession. The Bureau of the Census, Department of Commerce, Immigration and Naturalization Service and other agencies have tended to categorize translators and interpreters as non-professionals, making immigration of translators and interpreters to the U.S., as well as an accurate count of our ranks, difficult. Furthermore, the U.S. Congress, even when discussing legislation that would fund foreign language study, has yet to authorize any type of translator/interpreter training or continuing education programs strictly for translators.

Getting Ahead in the Profession

No doubt a major interest of every translator or interpreter is getting ahead, being a success. All translators who want to earn a living from the profession are concerned about making the most of their skills and abilities. As Snyder notes in this volume, one way to increase such opportunities is by conveying a professional attitude to the client. This means showing that translators are not the stereotypical ones many of us have seen depicted in cartoons, where the woman with a head covered with curlers is seated alongside a toaster, coffee cup in one hand and a pencil in the other, surrounded by dictionaries.

As Sherwin points out, local translator organizations can help individuals succeed as translators. She explains that one of the principal reasons why translators join local translator groups is in order to get ahead. They want to learn about technology, trends, and job opportunities. Contact with other translators is a help, as is a listing in a local group's translation services directory. Furthermore, as Ganser notes, a number of translators join special-interest groups to meet and gain contacts with others who have the same language combinations or subject matter interests. This too can bring access to contacts and to knowledge that will increase the skill level of the individual and opportunities for success.

Just what skills or credentials are useful in getting work and getting ahead is another on-going issue. As Bokor, Bierman and others note, no particular degree or license is needed in this country for translators and, to make matters more confusing, unlike most other professions, in many cases the client cannot readily judge the quality of the product. Therefore the question arises of just what types of credentials will be the most impressive to would-be clients. There seems little question that one reason so many translators have joined the ATA has been to take an accreditation exam. This is particularly true for translators trying to break into the market and who do not have a well-established client base. As Bierman notes, accreditation and certification are limited at this time to a finite number of languages. Furthermore, ATA accreditation is only recognized by the ATA as long as the person remains a member in good standing. Some translators have looked for alternatives and have gone to Canada to take the exam offered by the CTIC provincial associations, which is given in any language requested, or they have tried to establish standards in their own language combination. The matter continues to be a controversial one, especially for translators unable to get some kind of certification or accreditation at this time.

Benefiting from a Changing World

The globalization of the profession is also having an impact on the field. Now translators can take assignments from clients in other countries, thanks to advanced technologies. Although they have a wider potential market, their competition is becoming more intense, as U.S. clients can also call on translators overseas to do their work, often at much lower rates than in the U.S., and with a greater supply of translators in the less frequently taught languages in the U.S. Thus, the question of how to keep the work in the U.S. while expanding the client base will probably continue to be an issue for some time to come.

A related change in subject-matter demand could well come about, and certainly indications exist already, due to the signing of the North American Free Trade Agreement and other international trade agreements. More and more U.S. companies are setting up offices in Mexico and elsewhere abroad, which means that they need to have their manuals and other publications put into the languages of the countries in which they are operating. Those translators skilled in business, technical subjects and advertising may well find an increase in the opportunities for success. Just how to become part of this trend and how to go about increasing their job opportunities is of increasing interest to many translators and interpreters in the U.S. It is a topic that has been addressed by the Canadian Translators and Interpreters Council (CTIC) at its meeting in Banff, Canada in May 1994, at the Regional Center for North America's Congress in 1992 and at other language conferences.

As the political climate changes, so does the need for certain languages. Preparing to meet future demands presents an enormous challenge for those hoping to become translators and for those who want to ensure a source of income in years to come. For example, with the collapse of the Soviet Union, more documents in need of translation are appearing in languages of former Soviet states, such as Ukrainian, Estonian, Lithuanian, and Latvian. At the same time, that collapse has brought about a rapid decline in U.S. government translations of security-related documents from Russian. As a result, many translators are asking just what languages they should be studying or what areas of expertise might be particularly useful in the future. However, as seen in the Szablya article, the political changes can also mean increased opportunities for energetic translators who wish to combine their language expertise with their business or marketing skills. The case of Hungary which they describe is but one example. As noted by both the Szablyas and Ganser, though, knowledge of the two cultures is essential and presents new challenges for those wishing to succeed in this newer market.

Ethics and the Profession

Most associations have codes of ethical conduct to which their members are to adhere. As can be seen in the article by Bokor, for the American Translators Association, the Ethics Committee has often meant a source to contact when unable to get paid for a job done. Certainly other aspects of ethical conduct are present in the codes of the various associations, yet, as noted by Nicholson, all too often, there may be no written standards of ethical conduct. This means that certain standards of conduct are expected and the organization in question may not have felt it necessary to put them in writing. I recall that it was for that reason the ATA Board recommended removal from its Bylaws of a cause of expulsion, that of public denigration of a colleague without documentation. There may also be issues of confidentiality, using the names of the translator without permission, editing text without the knowledge of the translator and other business practices which are sometimes questioned on ethical if not legal grounds. Lack of prompt payment, confidentiality, use of names in advertising, speaking ill of the competition, making false claims, unethical advertising, knowing who owns the translation, what happens when a disk is submitted and redone without the translator's knowledge, are some of the problems that may arise, as explained by Maier, because there was no agreement between the translator and client. Because of such a failure to get it in writing, the translator may well end up seeking redress with an ethics committee, if not a court of law. For that reason Maier urges translators to get it all in writing before accepting a job and she provides a sample contract.

Putting Technology to Work

Many of us can remember that it was just a few years ago when we were using a typewriter to do our translations. Just a few years later clients were insisting on disks and then modems. I can recall meetings of a local translation group where some of the best known translators in the vicinity were bemoaning the fact that technology was going by them too fast and that they would never learn to use a computer, much less learn how to benefit from the latest technology.

One of the areas of relatively new technologies that arouses great emotions in some translators is that of machine translation. As noted by Vasconcellos in this volume, there are those who see machine translation as a threat to the profession and others who feel it can be a useful tool. Yet, few can deny that MT systems, albeit somewhat simple ones, are now within the reach of the average translator and could actually help increase productivity over time.

At the same time, how to get the most out of available technology is of key concern. Just where to get useful information and how to decide what to buy, when to wait, and how to learn of trends is something of interest to virtually all translators. In his article, Melby discusses some of the directions in which technology is going and provides some insights into the levels of technology of interest to the translator.

Needless to say, getting ahead by making the best use of technology possible is related to financial investment but also increased future economic success. More productivity can mean more income for the same amount of time that would have been spent on much less volume just a few years ago. And keeping abreast of new technologies can be a key factor.

Economic Issues

No discussion of issues of importance to translation professionals would be complete without a mention of economic concerns. Until the 1990s, discussions of the economic aspects of translation were commonplace. In its newsletter, the National Association of Judiciary Interpreters and Translators (NAJIT) published a list of prices its members should charge. The American Association of Language Specialists (TAALS) was devoted to better working conditions for its members. The American Translators Association had a Rate Guidelines Committee (RGC) that once a year published a list of fees that it recommended translators take into consideration. And it is likely that the RGC rates were reprinted or referred to by other translation associations.

In 1990 all of that changed. Virtually all major translator/interpreter associations in the U.S. became the target of anti-trust investigations by the Federal Trade Commission. By 1994, at least two of the organizations, TAALS and the American Society of Interpreters (ASI) had signed consent decrees in which the press has reported that they agreed, among other points, to halt any meeting at which two of those present mentioned rates. As for the ATA, the Association was notified by the FTC in March 1994 that the investigation had been closed. To its credit, the ATA Board had approved a strict anti-trust policy seven months before the FTC investigation began and this undoubtedly influenced the decision of the FTC not to prosecute the ATA or pursue the investigation further.

In short, it has become very difficult for organizations and individuals to discuss economic matters, thereby leaving many persons confused as to where they can get information on what they might expect to pay or charge for translations. Because of the legal implications of discussion of rates, this is one topic that has not been treated in detail in this book, even though it is no doubt at or near the top of the list of professional concerns.

A related on-going economic issue expressed by freelance translators who expect to earn a living from the profession has been what to do about the entry of newcomers willing to advertise cheap services or to undercut the competitor. It has become apparent through the FTC investigation that undercutting cannot be condemned but must be allowed. In fact, the ATA Board of Directors removed a phrase "will not engage in unfair business practices" from its Code of Professional Conduct because an FTC attorney, during the deposition procedure at which this guest editor was present, questioned whether that might mean that members were prohibited from charging less than their competitors. In fact, in 1994 the FTC gave permission to the American Medical Association to expel members engaged in price-gouging. Given the fact discussed earlier that many users of translations do not understand how much expertise may be required to produce an accurate work, the fact that the client is often in no position to judge the quality of the project, and the fact that translation is for many a way of moonlighting to make a few extra dollars, the entry of newcomers willing to work for little remuneration will probably be an issue for many translators for some time to come.

Another economic concern for some has to do with the freelance /bureau relationship, as some translators view themselves as exploited by the bureaus. Such terms as "translation coolie" have appeared in the ATA *Chronicle*, and I once read something written by a former Board member of the ATA who said that company bureau owners and supervisors had in common that they wanted the cheapest product with the fastest turnaround and that quality was not a concern. Fortunately not all translators feel this way, and many bureaus have very constructive and productive relations with the translators who do work for them. Yet a concern as whether agencies and individuals should both be members of the same association has come up as recently as 1993 in the ATA.

For translators who work in-house or who seek such positions, the trend would appear to be away from in-house staff and more toward contractors, provided translations are not being eliminated entirely for budgetary or other reasons. For the employer or user of translation services, there are certainly distinct advantages to an in-house staff as well as disadvantages. On the positive side, there is no need to keep on teaching format, terminology and other details that it is necessary to spell out to each new contractor. Staff members are available every day for work on the telephone, rush requests, oral translations and other work requiring an instant turn-around. And they can be given confidential work without any fear that the work will be divulged. On the other hand, the cost factor may lead employers to prefer contractors. When there is no work pending, there are no payments, including benefits, to an idle staff. When the volume is heavy, there need be no backlog because the work can be contracted out to as many translators as needed. And if the demand changes for particular languages, the shift in contractors can be made to utilize translators with the desired skills. Finally, those preferring contracting services might claim that productivity is greater, the turn-around time is less, since the translators are paid by the word rather than according to a salary that remains the same regardless of the speed with which the translator works.

To make matters worse, current tax laws, as applied to full and part-time freelances and to those who hire them, are going through a great deal of questioning, thus far to the financial detriment of translators. At the heart of much of the debate are the major changes in the home office deductions, explained in detail by Bierman.

The Role of Universities in Translator/Interpreter Training

As noted by Bowen, changes are taking place in perceptions of translating and interpreting. One reason is the change in generations of translators. After World War II, many translators entering the profession in this country were immigrants in search of a means of support, but the next generation of translators came predominantly from language majors born in the U.S., many of whom had lived overseas, who more or less fell into the profession as a way of using their language skills without having to devote them to teaching. Now a new generation of translators is emerging. Although many persons are still entering the profession in the traditional manner, more and more of them have had university translator training. As noted by Park, the number of universities offering translation courses has increased dramatically. At the same time, however, he remarks that most courses are just that, rather than part of an extensive degree program. Still, it could be said that such courses not only train potential translators but serve to discourage those who do not have the skills necessary to become successful translators.

Nevertheless, the role of the university is still controversial, particularly among translators themselves, as explained by Cordero. Those who have never taken any translation theory courses tend to be particularly disdainful of such offerings. Yet, the university does have a role in the professionalization of translation, as can be seen in the Cordero article. One contribution that this writer has seen is the requirement that students in translation programs do an internship in an office that provides translations. This first-hand experience provides the would-be translators with insight, gets them accustomed to working under pressure and to meeting deadlines, and allows them to concentrate on translation as a real job, not a university class.

Perhaps a further area of conflict is the fact that some of the most successful translators are not welcome on university campuses, as they lack the advanced degrees necessary to teach translation, particularly at the graduate level. On the other hand, those translators might note that in their opinion, all too often, translation classes are taught by professors who have agreed to teach them in order to gain more job security and not because they have any experience or knowledge in translation and the profession. In addition, a frequent criticism of university programs is that they often focus on translation of literature while the real need is for technical translators. However, as noted by Bowen, teaching translation of literature is not necessarily bad.

There are many who would say that translators are not made but are born, that no program can create a really good translator if he or she does not have a certain amount of talent. Furthermore, as Cordero shows, certain controversy exists regarding the usefulness of theory classes as part of a translator-training program. Personally, I would say that had I had the benefit of some formal training in translation I might have saved myself years of what was to be, more than anything, a self-teaching process.

The university can also serve as a center for continuing education. Many translators, even if they have been working in the profession for some time, still want to know what their colleagues do regarding editing the original text, when they improve it or translate what they find (not what might have been meant), or when to call the requester to educate him about the content, especially for materials created in-house. Ganser talks about the need for an understanding of business. In any case, most translators sooner or later find themselves in need of some continuing education, whether through literature or workshops, conferences or the classroom. The question is where such training can be found and whether it is worthwhile and affordable. As previously noted, grants or government-sponsored workshops are all too rare, which means that in many cases those organizing such sessions tend to do so with the cooperation of local universities.

Acknowledgements

As the guest editor for this volume, I would like to express my gratitude to Marilyn Gaddis Rose, Editor of the Series, for her patience and suggestions during the process of assembling this volume, and to the contributors for their willingness to take the time and effort to share with us their expertise and experience in areas of interest to translators and interpreters. It is because of such dedicated individuals that we may all move forward in our chosen profession.

Section 1:

Achieving Success as a Language Professional

The Paradox of Professionalism

Nancy Snyder

People want different things out of life. Some people focus on money, some on recognition and others on family and relationships. Personal motivation is partly influenced by the culture we grow up in.

Management books will tell you that if you want to reward and motivate an employee, you need to consider the generation that employee comes from. In the generation that came of age in the forties and fifties, you offer a shot at overtime—a chance to work longer hours and make more money. For people who came of age in the sixties and early seventies, you offer time off—time to enjoy life and be creative. And for people coming of age in the eighties and nineties you offer cold, hard cash—a cash bonus.

More often than not, if you ask a person who does not have his or her own business why he/she would like to have their own business, the answer you will get is "to be my own boss." Or "to be independent," "set my own hours" or a similar variation on this theme.

Now, this longing for independence and freedom, a longing to structure your own quality of life is a common desire, especially among those of us who came of age in the sixties. Life is not about nine to five, life is what happens to you while you are busy making other plans. The opposite of the nine to five routine, a totally optional lifestyle with the freedom to choose, is what I like to call leading the gypsy life.

This paper will not have too much to say to the people who grew up prior to the sixties. Those people are more familiar with using good manners and consistent hard work to ensure success. The target audience of this paper is more likely people who are looking to lead the gypsy life or get instant financial gratification. But it wouldn't hurt to read it anyway, just in case any of it fits. Unfortunately, a lot of what I have to say is like talking about those touchy subjects that even your best friend won't bring up.

The topic of this paper is professionalism. *Webster's New World Dictionary of the American Language* gives several definitions of the word professional, and we will discuss three of them.

One definition reads "engaged in a specified occupation for pay or as a means of livelihood: as, a professional writer." We are going to be talking about professional translators—people who are engaged in translation for pay, and in particular as a means of livelihood.

Another definition also applies to translators: "making some activity not usually followed for gain, such as a sport, the source of one's livelihood." Now, since translation is an activity often followed for gain, we need to paraphrase the definition to read "making an activity that would be followed, even if it did not result in gain, such as an art, the source of one's livelihood." I think a lot of us would be translating for fun even if we never made a cent. Long before we ever got paid for translating, most of us were probably working on a translation project for the joy of it.

The third definition we will discuss is "of, engaged in, or worthy of the high standards of, a profession." The key words here are "high standards."

Now, to put them all together, I will give you my definition of a professional translator: "A person who makes translation, an activity they love, the source of his or her livelihood by engaging in and being worthy of the high standards of the profession."

Perhaps it seems that our discussion of Webster's has taken us far away from the concept of the gypsy life that was described at the beginning. So, to recap, let me present my definition of a person leading the gypsy life: "A person who spends time doing something he/she loves while enjoying quality of life, personal independence and growth and the flexibility to create his or her desired lifestyle by choosing working hours, choosing pleasant working relationships with people of his or her choice in a location that he/she enjoys (and who still has enough money to eat and pay rent)."

From my five years of experience as a self-employed person, I can assure you that this kind of life style is most definitely attainable. But do most self-employed people attain this life style? No, they do not. Out of all new business starts, something like 85% fail within the first two years. Now, a lot of things can go wrong when you are starting a business. But considering that so many people express "to be my own boss, to be independent, make my own hours" as a reason for going into business, my hunch is that many, many of these business fail for that reason. People start a business because they want to lead the gypsy life and then the business fails because they lead the gypsy life instead of tending to business.

One of my clients said to me recently, "You know, you're not only the most professional person I work with, you're the only really professional person I work with."

You just won't believe the stories I hear from her. When she is looking for freelancers, she sends out sample translations to people who have expressed an interest in working for her. Many of those samples are never returned or even acknowledged. When she does find people she can work with, she gets late work, sloppy work, and sometimes no work at all returned by the due date. When a job is overdue and she calls to check on the job status, sometimes the translator doesn't even answer the phone. And sometimes if they do, they give a flimsy excuse like "I'm sorry, I had it almost done and then the cat got sick and I had to take her to the vet." (I am making up this excuse to ensure confidentiality, but the actual excuse was equally lame.) Sometimes people treat her as if they are doing her a favor, as if they know her field better than she does, or they just try to fake their way through when they know they don't know the subject area or the terminology. Or sometimes they want her to take the responsibility for their business and tell them what to charge, whether or not to charge for faxing, how to work their modem, etc., etc., etc.

What's wrong with this picture? Well, just imagine that you have taken your car to the shop and when you go back at the time agreed upon to pick it up, they haven't even started it. Or they say they couldn't get it done because it's hunting season and they got a doe permit this year. Or that they don't know if they can fix it, but anyway it's actually your own fault because you have bad driving habits. Or what if you took the car in and the mechanic asked you what brand of oil he/she should use? If any one of these things happened, do you think you would take it back to that shop again? I wouldn't. Now, let's raise the stakes a little and imagine it is the personnel at a doctor's office that gives you these kinds of excuses or asks you to tell them what medicine to prescribe for you or doesn't seem to know what they are doing. Are you going back? I think not.

The kinds of unprofessional behaviors we are talking about are behaviors that most of us would simply not tolerate in someone we wanted to do business with. How ironic that many small business people, by trying to attain the gypsy life, simply ruin their businesses by unprofessional behavior.

I claimed above that the gypsy life is actually attainable. But the paradox is that the only way the gypsy life of freedom, flexibility and chosen lifestyle can be obtained is by a serious, long-term investment in professionalism. The kind of professionalism in the definition that reads "worthy of the high standards of a profession."

Not too long ago, someone sold a lot of books by claiming that he had learned everything he needed to know in kindergarten. Sometimes the most obvious things in life need to be highlighted and pondered. The discussion that follows of high professional standards may seem painfully obvious, but from what I hear from my friend, translators with high professional standards are in the minority in her experience. So I offer these suggestions for improving professionalism, at the risk of being dubbed the "Miss Manners" of the translation profession. Actually I would consider that quite a compliment. Miss Manners' underlying philosophy is that manners are not empty formality, they are behaviors that we use out of consideration to put people at ease socially. Professional manners are behaviors that we use to put our clients at ease, thereby promoting their eagerness to deal with us in a long term business relationship.

Most of the points listed below don't really have anything to do with translation. And except for one about accuracy, these are not suggestions on how to improve your work. If you already have all the work you need and you are making the kind of money you want by holding on to your good clients, you will not need these suggestions. But if you are finding that clients are hard to get or hard to hold onto, they merit your consideration. These are suggestions on how to improve your professionalism.

1. Know yourself.

Make sure you know what you are being asked to do and whether or not you can do it.

2. Know what you are doing.

Does the customer pay for delivery or is delivery one of your business costs? If your material is going to be edited and changes have to be made to the files, will you make the changes or will the changes be made by the agency? It's your business, and you make the rules. This doesn't mean there is no room for negotiation, but it does mean that you need to make up your own mind about your standard policies for services you offer to the client. If you don't know what policies are best, brainstorm with some of your colleagues, but don't expect your client to teach you how to run a business.

3. Be honest.

If you are asked to do something outside your area of expertise, admit you can't do it if that is the case. You may want to subcontract to someone else or give a referral. Customers appreciate your help when you give referrals for work you can't do and will also appreciate your honesty about your skills. If you can do the job, but there are a few terms that you absolutely can not come up with despite your exhaustive research efforts, ask for help. But don't call every hour or two with a word you can't find in one dictionary. You will need to do your own research—at a research library or by networking with colleagues. Contact the client only after you have exhausted these avenues. There are terms that are corporate jargon that you won't be able to get anywhere but from the client. But do your homework first.

4. Be accurate.

Proofread your work. I used to think I was very accurate. And I did proofread. But then I had an opportunity to work with a wonderfully professional woman who edited my work and pointed out some stupid mistakes that were still there after I had proofread and thought I was done. She introduced me to the concept of the "quality control read through." After you are completely, finally, ultimately finished with a document, read it one last time. I guarantee you will find a couple more mistakes that you missed the last three times through it.

5. Be neat.

This applies to your personal appearance, which we will discuss below, but it also applies to every job you do and every piece of correspondence you produce to send to a client. If your customer sees a misspelled letter typed with a bad ribbon over chunks of white out, how do you think you can convince him/her that you will do an accurate job of translating the critical specifications the company needs to design and build a project costing hundreds of thousands of dollars?

6. Use a separate phone line for business if you work at home.

Since translation is not yet a profession that is well understood in this country, it is sometimes hard to get people to take us seriously as professionals to begin with. You are only adding a strike against yourself if your customer hears pots and pans rattling when you answer the phone. The customer thinks "just what I expected, a housewife with a hobby. She couldn't possibly understand our technology." Do not let your children answer the phone for you, and if they are not going to be quiet when you are on the phone, answer the phone in another room. Now, I am a mother and truthfully, the bottom line is that motherhood is more important to me than business. But you will never catch me letting my customers know that, because when I am working for them, they have my undivided attention. I have a beautiful daughter. And I'm sure that your children are delightful, too. But your customer does not want to deal with them. Even I, a doting mother, begin to doubt the seriousness of a person I am talking with on the phone who keeps getting interrupted by children while we are talking business or who tells me that something that was promised is late because of a child's activities.

7. Dress like a professional.

Now, you can get rebellious about this if you want. You can say that dress as a social convention is a straight jacket of society and that as a self-employed person, no boss is going to tell you what to wear or enforce a dress code on you. But this is another example of trying to attain the gypsy life by leading the gypsy life. Isn't it worthwhile to get a good suit and wear it for two hours a week meeting with clients if it helps you to make enough sales to sit and work on the patio in your cut-offs sipping a cool drink for the other 38 hours a week?

8. Be friendly.

If there are several qualified people available for a job, and one is always abrupt, crabby and irritable on the phone and the other is always friendly and has something nice to say, which one would you call if you were handing out the work? Your customer has pressures of his or her own. So don't let your own pressures interfere with your business relationships. Put a smile on your lips and some honey in your voice when you pick up that phone.

9. But don't get too personal.

If you seem outgoing and are a good listener, your customers may tell you about their work hassles. This is not totally professional, but we are not making up tips for your customer, we are thinking of things to help you. This does not entitle you to start unloading your gripes. Does your hairdresser or bartender listen to how you feel? Of course. Do you want to hear how your bartender or hairdresser feels? Probably not, because you are paying him or her, so it feels as if it should be your time. This doesn't mean you can never say anything personal to customers. A little personal conversation can help develop a rapport. Just keep it light and positive and not too personal.

10. Honor commitments.

If you say you are going to do something, do it. If you cannot do it, don't commit yourself. If you find that you have committed yourself to something you later find out is impossible, contact the person you have made the commitment to immediately and explain the difficulty in honoring the commitment.

11. The customer is always right.

Of course, this saying is not absolutely true. The customer may sometimes make a mistake or be wrong, and you may need to point that out tactfully. But this old adage is a shorthand way of saying that the customer always deserves your respect. For that matter, the customer always deserves your gratitude. Without your customer's money, you don't eat, and you don't have a roof over your head. The customer does not owe you gratitude or appreciation, the customer owes you nothing except to pay the bill on time. It's nice if you do get compliments, but that is a bonus, not your due.

12. Be patient.

The customer is in the business of his or her choice, and you are in the translation business. You probably know more about translation than your customer ever will. But this is no reason to be arrogant. Your customer may ask questions that show a lack of knowledge and seem stupid to you. When ignorant questions come up, you must keep your cool and remind yourself that this is your opportunity to promote understanding of the translation profession in America. A rude or arrogant answer will not help your customer to learn. It will only confirm his or her suspicion that translators are difficult to deal with. It may be a good idea to rehearse some answers for typical questions so you won't be taken aback when they come up. I offer here two answers that I have used for the two most frequent questions asked by customers who don't understand translation. I guess they are pretty effective, because after using them, I have still gotten the jobs. When the customer says, "Charge by the word? Even the little words like 'a' or 'the'? You mean I have to pay the same amount of money for 'a' that I pay for 'piezoelectric'?," I respond, "Well look at it this way. If you have an examination from your dentist, you are paying for the totality of his or her knowledge and expertise. You will not get a discount from the fee if some of your teeth do not have cavities." Or if the customer says, "Well, if you know German, then why on earth can't you translate into German instead of only into English?" with a snort that I suspect means that the customer seriously doubts whether I actually do know German, I try to get the person to understand the concept of active vs. passive knowledge with this example. "Suppose you read a book on the space program (or some other but newsworthy but very technical topic). There will be a number of technical terms. You may have to look a couple up, but most you will understand from context well enough to understand the concepts and even explain them to a friend. But it is highly unlikely that you will use the technical terms from the book. You will understand them, but not necessarily be able to reproduce them when you want to because they are part of your *passive* knowledge. This is similar to my situation when translating German. I understand the German terms and the concepts they represent. I am able to express them actively in English, my native language. But the German terms are part of my passive knowledge that I am not able to produce on demand well enough to ensure quality translations into German."

13. Be humble.

Your customer probably knows more about his or her business than you ever will. Sometimes your job may involve listening carefully to find out how you can best help the customer to do what he/she already knows from experience is best.

14. Be tolerant of differences.

Your customer knows what the people in the shop or the people in the front office call their brand of widgets. Maybe the last company you worked for spelled them "widgets." But if this new company wants it spelled "widgettes" to add a continental flair, give them what they want. It's important to be accurate, but constantly insisting that your way is the only right way does not make you appear more knowledgeable, it only puts the customer off.

15. Be sympathetic.

You may have been in this business a long time. You know how important translation is, you know how to judge a good quality translation and you are aware of the effort involved and skill required, which justify your price. Your customer may be a person who has never dealt with translation before. He/she doesn't have a clue about how to find a good translator or what it costs to get a good quality translation. I've said it before and I'll say it again—oftentimes the inexperienced customer views us as a homeowner views a plumber. You never plan for a plumbing emergency; you probably don't know where to find a good plumber. Since you can't do the work yourself, you don't understand what is involved, and the price is always way too high because you never budgeted for it in the first place. Imagine yourself as a homeowner in this situation and then imagine an arrogant plumber who does not treat you politely. Once you can imagine how that would feel, you can begin to have a little sympathy for your clients. They may be pressured to make a decision about an unbudgeted expense. Give them the information needed patiently and if they gasp at the price you can even respond to that issue sympathetically. You can address the fact that your fee may sound high because they have not been in a position to need this service before and you can clarify for them the importance of translation and the importance of translation quality. But don't get angry with them because the price sounds high to them. It is a natural response for people unfamiliar with buying translation services.

This professional attitude is pretty demanding, isn't it? Well, yes, these high professional standards will take some self-examination to consider and some effort to implement. But the paradox is that after a consistent application of professional practices, you will be in a position to lead the gypsy life. You will have an almost limitless income potential, or you can limit your income and your work hours so you can devote your time to family, a hobby or any other goal that is worthwhile to you. You can wear what you want, work where you want, work with people you like or be alone, plan your vacations when you want, get up when you want and eat when you want. Then there are also the finer points of the gypsy life for the true connoisseur to consider: you could get a laptop computer and work on the patio or at the beach or even equip your RV with an office and lead a Nomadic life. The world and your lifestyle can be completely open to you. And all it takes is a committed investment in professionalism.

The Value of Local Translator Groups

ANN C. SHERWIN

In August 1985, six translators gathered around my dining-room table over lunch—four active ATA members, a self-declared loner, and a beginner—to consider the formation of a local translators group. As the sole "survivor" of that pioneer group (the others either didn't follow through or have since gone their separate ways), I am nonetheless happy to report that the Carolina Association of Translators and Interpreters (CATI) is alive and well today as a chapter of the American Translators Association. Our current directory lists over 200 members, we have group meetings monthly in four metropolitan areas, as well as an annual conference, and our leadership has enjoyed a healthy turnover. Through concerted public relations efforts, we have gained widespread recognition as a contact point for the translation profession in North and South Carolina.

Similar stories exist all over the United States, as translators seek to personalize their relationship to that large, diverse, and remote entity known as the American Translators Association. As a result, ATA is now an immediate supportive presence for thousands of translators engaged in what is otherwise essentially solitary work.

The fostering of local and regional translator groups through the Chapters Committee is, in my opinion, ATA's most effective means of outreach to the working translator. Because chapters and cooperating groups, ATA's two types of official affiliates, can also accept members not affiliated with the national association, ATA has a much larger constituency than its actual membership figures reflect. Its influence extends even beyond the local group, in that local activities are normally open to visitors and newsletters communicate to prospective members and advertisers as well.

Translators with little or no collegial contact at the national level may tend to think of their association in the third rather than the first person. My premise is that we, the individual members, and we, the chapters and cooperating groups, are ATA in its most vital form. Instead of sitting back and waiting for an illusory "them" to do things for us, we need to see ourselves as the grass roots of the association, as ATA at work in the field.

For the sake of brevity, I shall refer to ATA chapters and cooperating groups as "local groups." Keep in mind, however, that some have a statewide or regional focus, and most welcome members outside their defined geographic boundaries. Much of what is said here also applies to translator groups not officially affiliated with ATA.

When translators were asked in a survey what professional issues of major concern to them were addressed more effectively at the local level, they named virtually every concern that ATA has ever attempted to address, and more: job contacts and referrals; information exchange on local economic conditions, markets, industries, resources; networking and collaboration; interaction with state and local governments; state certification; public relations, client education, and professional recognition; recruitment, training, continuing education and technical support; mediation services; lobbying; collective advertising—the list goes on.

Because of its greater accessibility, the local group is seen as an excellent source of help. Both beginning translators and working translators at all levels of experience tap it for job leads, terminology, general advice, and moral support.

The local group also plays a key role in making the ATA accreditation program a reality, for it is here that most accreditation workshops and examination sittings are organized. Nearly all local groups offer at least two sittings a year, which are open to all ATA members willing to travel to the site in question.

National committees and projects come and go, depending on who has the time and energy to work on them. Because ATA leaders are scattered from coast to coast, the wheels move slowly, often at considerable expense of both time and money. At the local level, members can meet more often and mobilize faster. Tasks are less formidable and the results more immediate and visible.

The Survey

In order to base this paper on more than my own experience, I invited all local groups that participate in the ATA Newsletter Exchange to take part in the aforementioned survey. Of the 67 completed questionnaires received, the Northern California Translators Association (NCTA) accounted for nearly half—they made their questionnaires stand out by using chartreuse paper! The rest are not distinguishable by locality unless the respondent provided an address, but collectively they came from the Austin Area Translators and Interpreters Association (AATIA), Carolina Association of Translators and Interpreters (CATI), Colorado Translators Association (CTA), Northern Ohio Translators Association (NOTA), and Northwest Translators and Interpreters Society (NOTIS), all but the first being an official affiliate of ATA at this time.

The main part of the survey was not highly structured. While multiple-choice questions or checklists would have made it easier to compile and analyze the results, the free-expression format brought out ideas I might not have thought of, which was its main purpose. As a frame of reference, the survey also included a more objective respondent-profile section. Here an overwhelming majority of the respondents identified themselves as independent translators of scientific, technical, commercial and/or legal material. Six respondents were (or had been at some time) salaried translators, eight did literary translation, and seven specialized in the humanities. Years of experience ranged from 0 to 27 (part-time years counted half) and years of membership ranged from 0 to 24 in ATA and 0 to 13 in a local group.

The profile section also included questions about the extent of the respondent's participation in a translator group, which yielded an "involvement" score. Based on a possible 21 points (8 for participation and 13 for service), the respondent's group involvement was rated as high (15-21 points), moderate (8-14), or low (7 or less). Fifty-seven per cent of the respondents scored low, but many of these were newcomers who had not had much time to earn involvement points. No one made it into the moderate-involvement group on participation alone. Service could be anything from tending a refreshment table to contributing a newsletter article or presenting a program. Extra weight was given to elective positions, editorships, and committee chairmanships held. Everyone scored at least two participation points, which they could get just by reading the newsletter regularly, or by occasionally attending a meeting and occasionally reading the newsletter.

Survey participants were first asked to identify their major concerns as an active or aspiring professional translator or interpreter. Some understood "concerns" in terms of worry and therefore focused on problems they faced. Others interpreted it in a broader sense: issues of professional concern to them. In either case, most responses fell into one of four major categories:

- economic factors
- professional recognition
- information exchange
- quality of work

Of course there is overlap. Professional recognition has economic implications, and the exchange of information among translators can affect virtually all aspects of our work, including quality.

Economic Factors

Nearly half the respondents (31) named economic concerns. The two most often mentioned were the need for more clients and the need for information regarding earnings potential. Though several respondents expressed interest in machine translation, only one expressed it in a way that suggested economic concern: "Will machines replace people?" Another sole respondent mentioned a need for health, disability and other insurance at group rates.

Interestingly, 14 of the 15 responses pertaining to remuneration came from the San Francisco Bay area (NCTA), where the cost of living is relatively high and the business environment very competitive. On the whole, California translators are probably under more economic pressure than their colleagues in the South and Midwest who took part in the survey, and many would like to see their local association do more to address this problem. Their concern should in no way be construed as a call for rate agreements or restraint of trade, but simply as a request for information about the economic realities of their work, such as is often made available for other industries through commissioned surveys.

Respondents also felt that local groups must continually call government and public attention to the economic advantages of keeping business local rather than sending it out of state or even overseas. Translators in all regions want more work, be they newcomers eager to build a clientele or experienced translators feeling the effects of the recession. Those who suffer no shortage of work would still like more in their fields of expertise. One respondent, dissatisfied with subcontract work, is concerned about finding direct clients without violating the trust of the bureaus he has worked for.

The good news is that active participation in a local translator group stimulates business. Survey participants who had been active in the profession before joining a local translator group were asked how their professional life had changed since they joined. One wrote that business had "picked up incredibly." Another said that name recognition gained through her leadership in the local group had brought her business. A third said that while her work had decreased since her move to a different state, referrals from the new local group helped keep her active. Local group affiliation enabled at least one independent translator to establish a bureau. It also enhanced business for many respondents indirectly:

"It's a great credential when I present myself to new customers."

"It has increased my visibility and helped me be more aggressive in getting jobs."

"I have more choices now."

"Inquiries come from farther afield."

"My work is more diverse."

When asked to name the single greatest benefit of membership in an ATA chapter or other local/regional group, two respondents mentioned referrals from colleagues and eight mentioned the listing in the local group's directory. While the 35 who named networking or contact with other translators probably had information exchange and collegial fellowship in mind, referrals and job leads are certainly a recognized benefit of networking.

Ten respondents stated that their professional life had not changed significantly since joining a local translator group. Another, while acknowledging some change, expressed disappointment that membership had not led to more jobs. Not surprisingly, nine of these, including the latter, had low group involvement scores. Paying dues to get a directory listing and skimming the newsletter occasionally are obviously not enough.

One respondent raised an important question: "I tend to rely more on the group than try to make my own connections: a mistake?" Yes! The association cannot do your marketing for you. Only after you've worked hard and established your reputation will business start falling into your lap on a regular basis—if you're lucky. But active participation can help you sharpen your skills, presentation, and business savvy, which in turn will enhance your salability. Attendance at meetings and workshops, service on boards or committees, and contributions to the newsletter (even if you live too far away to attend meetings) show that you are serious about your profession.

Professional Recognition

Survey participants also raised two closely related concerns of many translators: personal recognition as a professional, and the image of the profession as a whole. Of the many definitions of "profession," here is a time-honored one from *Webster's Third New International* (1986) with which I sense translators want to be identified:

> A calling requiring specialized knowledge and often long and intensive preparation including instruction in skills and methods as well as in the scientific, historical, or scholarly principles underlying such skills and methods, maintaining by force of organization or concerted opinion high standards of achievement and conduct, and committing its members to continued study and to a kind of work which has for its prime purpose the rendering of a public service.

As translators, we want the public, particularly our clients, to know that our work requires a high level of skill that not all bilingual persons possess. As an organization, we strive to maintain high standards of achievement and conduct while still maintaining an open membership policy. Through continuing education programs we demonstrate our commitment to study. Finally, the primary purpose of our work, facilitation of international and intercultural communication, is without doubt an indispensable public service.

Several respondents want their group to do more in the realm of "client education"—a term that I use reluctantly. Regardless how we feel about our clients' limited understanding of our work, in my opinion, we stand to gain more favor by dispensing "information" rather than "education." Our public relations efforts should focus not on our own virtues but on the needs and concerns of our clients. When we beat our drums too hard, we're seen as just another self-serving special-interest group. If we downplay our own interests and concentrate on those of our client or the public at large, we are more likely to come across as professionals in the sense of Webster's definition.

Local groups can establish speakers' bureaus and develop informative materials tailored to special markets in their area. CATI publishes a brochure entitled "Translation: Your Access to the World," which members can purchase at cost to distribute along with their business cards. NOTA produced a promotional video some years back. Many groups have booths at trade fairs and other public events. Thoughtful, well-written letters from the association to newspaper editors generate public respect, as do carefully chosen pro-bono service projects.

Information Exchange

Nearly every respondent acknowledged the value of exchanging information with colleagues—about economic factors already discussed, as well as about business protocol, bureau/subcontractor relations, improving efficiency, finding the right terminology, and problem solving. Many survey respondents listed specific topics on which they would like more information or were prepared to share information, such as how to negotiate effectively, use a modem, explore a prospective equipment purchase, evaluate a dictionary, figure charges, market skills locally, organize business records, edit their own work. They want to know about computer software, terminology resources, industry trends, and especially developments in machine translation. They want nuts-and-bolts answers to questions like "What makes a good or bad translation?"

Translators share information at local meetings, workshops and conferences, in publications, and on computer bulletin boards. NCTA publishes "A Practical Guide for Translators," a booklet specifically geared to the San Francisco Bay area but useful to any translator. A great deal of information flows informally, as colleagues get to know each other in social settings or pick up the phone when a pressing question arises. A respondent whose major concern was finding the *proper* terminology for every job, wrote "Translators in the same language combination but with different fields support each other. We are just a local call away!"

Through the ATA newsletter exchange, published information reaches a much wider audience. Mutual permission to reprint items (under certain restrictions) is part of the exchange agreement. Many local groups circulate the exchange publications among interested members and then store the collection, along with other library materials, in a place that is accessible to members. It can also be useful to exchange publications with other organizations having overlapping interests, such as international trade associations, foreign-language teachers' associations, cross-cultural interest groups, writers' groups and nonprofit umbrella organizations.

The local group is a meeting ground where experienced translators can share their knowledge with newcomers. Beginners look forward to this when they join, and it was my primary motive for starting a group where none existed, when I was still a beginner. The benefits to newcomers are obvious, but seasoned veterans also regard the sharing of knowledge as a professional development opportunity. You may have heard it said that you don't really know a subject until you try to teach it. Presenting a program or leading a workshop is always a learning experience for me. Not only does it motivate me to fill my own knowledge gaps in the subject; it also gives me valuable practice in analyzing and organizing information and in public speaking. Communication skills developed in the less pressured atmosphere of a CATI meeting help me project a better image to clients as well.

Two long-time active members said that their local groups tended to cater to the novice more than the veteran translator, and that they had to go to the national level to get the kind of information and professional support they needed. They stated this merely as a difference rather than as a criticism. However group leaders should take note. If you continually neglect the needs of experienced translators, you will find it increasingly harder to recruit and retain them.

Quality

Of course information is not an end in itself. It is a means to many ends, including a major concern of the high-involvement group: the quality of their service. Of the 14 respondents in this group, all but one (93%) mentioned major concerns directly related to the quality of their work or service, whereas only 53% of the moderately involved and 26% of the least involved members expressed concern about quality. It is of course debatable which variable is the cause and which the effect. Naturally people concerned about quality are likely to pursue opportunities to improve not only their own work but the standards of the profession as a whole. People who join a professional association for other reasons also become more conscious of quality through interaction with colleagues.

An interesting observation is that there was very little overlap between respondents who listed finding clients as a major concern and those who listed quality-related issues. Only four listed both. The same was true of the overlap between remuneration and quality, but it was a different four. These eight persons appear to recognize a correlation between quality and economic rewards. Of course if the question had been presented in a different way, e.g., as a checklist, everyone would probably have checked quality. What self-respecting translator would admit to not caring about quality?

Quality-minded translators care about all aspects of their work. They want to understand their subject matter fully and to translate using correct terminology, grammar and style. They want to increase their efficiency, so that they can meet tighter deadlines without compromising quality. They want the finished product to look good and the client to be fully satisfied.

Some local groups address the quality issue through published articles. For more concrete help, they may maintain a resource library or facilitate the sharing of member-owned resources, e.g., through terminology banks or dictionary pools. The primary vehicle, however, is continuing education. Survey participants expressed enthusiasm for the continuing education events already offered locally, but they want more. Two respondents expressed a desire for more advanced training.

Continuing education may be in the form of mini-classes presented at regular meetings, such as the Fora Linguarum offered by the Mid-America Chapter of the American Translators Association (MICATA). It may be a conference, workshop or other special event. It may be a field trip to a local industrial site. Translators who work with uncommon languages appreciate continuing education programs from which they can benefit even if no one else is present who works with their language pair. If a group offers programs geared only to the major languages, translators of other languages may drift away.

Other Issues

There are several issues that only one or two people listed as major concerns, but which I sense are important to others from their overall comments. For instance, the respondent who listed "helping to promote understanding" as a major concern probably spoke for many of us.

Personal job satisfaction was mentioned only twice. But considering how many translators love their work despite limited economic prospects and perceived prestige, it must be an important issue. The role of the local group in job satisfaction is largely one of support and fellowship—a fringe benefit mentioned or implied by the vast majority of respondents. It is easier to appreciate the less tangible rewards of our profession in the stimulating company of international people who share our passion for language. Also many respondents find great personal satisfaction in helping others. After all, probably the only way we can "repay" those who helped us along the way is to pass it on.

Another issue that surely concerns more than the two who mentioned it is time management. This is a common problem for self-employed people, especially those whose work is not confined to traditional business hours. Translators conditioned to accepting almost any work they could get as fledglings may find it hard to turn away business once they have all they can handle. Work begins to encroach on family time, social life, household duties, and personal leisure. Add in the pressure on busy translators to be leaders in their professional associations, and burnout becomes a real danger. Articles and programs on time management can help, but local groups also need to spread the work around, and especially to tap the energies of enthusiastic newcomers who may not have so many demands on their time yet.

Only one respondent mentioned promotion of the profession to students, but this is an important concern. Despite the advent of machine translation, the world will always need talented human linguists as well. Like ATA, most local groups offer reduced membership fees to students. But to cultivate a generation of successors and ensure the survival of our profession at its best, we should also send informed representatives to speak to high-school and college foreign-language classes and to participate in career days. While most groups would do this if asked, a few actively solicit such invitations.

The local group is an outlet for translator activists, according to these responses:

"I have served on the chapter Board, and this has given me an opportunity to work on issues I care about, e.g., translator-client relations and ethics."

"I have polished my PR skills as group spokesperson."

"My membership in the local group and regional chapter has ... [provided] me with a platform for my energy and ideas."

"Being active in the local/regional group has served as a bridge between going it alone and working at the national level."

Conclusions

When I developed the survey, I expected to find correlations between the extent of respondents' group involvement and their answers to other questions. My hypothesis was admittedly altruistic: that you benefit from an activity in proportion to what you put into it. The informal survey confirmed my expectations, but more importantly, it identified many aspects of our profession that can and should be addressed collectively. If you are already active in an ATA chapter or cooperating group, I hope the ideas, experience and opinions summarized here will help you guide your group in even more productive directions. If you are not yet associated with a local translator group, the ATA headquarters staff or the head of the Chapters Committee can help you make the connection. The American Translators Association will be as effective at the local level as *we* choose to make it!

Getting it in Writing: The Key to Problem-Free Business Relationships

JANE MAIER

A close colleague who is an excellent translator from English into French called yesterday to complain about an agency which had just cancelled a project for which he had set aside two weeks to work on, turning down several other assignments in order to work on theirs. Two weeks ago, the owner of a new agency called to ask if she was justified in reducing the agreed-upon pay to a translator who had turned in a "lousy" translation, which required many hours of revising and a few sleepless nights. These types of complaints are not the exception in this day and age. On the contrary, they are on the rise.

A survey of inquiries made to ATA's Ethics Committee reveals some recurrent common problems: 3/4 of the complaints were from translators who hadn't been paid or whose invoices were overdue, with most of the remaining complaints about deductions being made from pay because of alleged errors in the translation or missed deadlines. Cancellation of projects with partial or no payment and word count disputes were among the other complaints received. These examples illustrate only too well the fact that most client-translator controversies arise from a lack of clear understanding of the terms of the agreement between them. (In this article, the term "client" means a direct client as well as a translation bureau.) Translators could save themselves a lot of time, money, and headaches if they would do one thing: Get some kind of document *in writing* stating both the client's and the translator's expectations BEFORE starting any translation job.

In these days when documents (including legally valid, signed agreements) can be sent instantly via fax machines, there really is no excuse for the client and translator not to confirm the terms of a job in writing. To help ATA members with this task, in 1989 I drew up, with the assistance of an attorney, a Model Contract for Translators. This contract was originally printed in the April 1989 issue of the *ATA Chronicle*, with a revised version based on member suggestions printed in the November/December 1989 issue. After some fine tuning and a final review by the attorney, printed copies of the Model Contract were available to attendees of ATA's Annual Conference in Salt Lake City, Utah in October 1991. For reference it is included at the end of this article.

In most cases, it seems that at best, translators receive a simple cover letter or fax of transmittal from their client, specifying only two things: price and deadline. But even those two points may not be completely clear. Is the price based on source language or target language word count? If the deadline is "five days from the date the document is received," is it five working days or five calendar days? What if the translator gets sick?

Besides specifying the details of price and deadline, a written agreement should contain a number of other things:

1. A description of the job and exactly what is included

A detailed statement of what the price includes is extremely important to avoid misunderstandings. It should answer the following:

Does the translation need to follow exactly the format of the original? Formatted text (especially tables) can take much longer to produce than straight word processed text.
Are editing and proofreading included?
Re-alphabetization of alphetized lists and indexes?
Paste-up of graphics?
Re-entry of equations?
Do columns of numbers need to be reproduced?
How will duplicated passages be charged?

2. Method and format of delivery

The contract should refer to the following:

Will the translation be returned by fax, modem or overnight courier?
Should it be in hard copy or on diskette?
In which software?
Formatted for IBM—or Macintosh?
What size disk?
High or low density?

3. Payment terms

In addition to price, you should specify exactly what is included and how it is to be paid (by the word, by the hour or by the piece). In addition, you should consider the following:

For large jobs, will you receive progress payments?
How often and what amount?
Are rush fees justified?
What exactly constitutes "rush"?
What about late payment terms? It is interesting to note that in complaints received by ATA's Ethics Committee about non-payment or slow payment, the related documentation (work orders, invoices, etc.) almost never includes payment terms or schedules, though it is not uncommon for translators to add late charges (!!). In my mind, this is not the way to establish a good on-going client-translator relationship!

4. Cancellation

This is one point I have rarely seen covered outside the Model Contract, yet is particularly important for large jobs. A translator may set aside a substantial amount of time and turn down other assignments in order to take on a translation promised by a client in the near future. If the project is cancelled before it is started, or even when the translator is part-way through it, he or she can suffer significant financial loss. For this reason, it may be a good idea to include a cancellation clause in the agreement, which specifies either that payment will be based on a prorated amount corresponding to the actual work completed and/or a certain percentage of the total contract amount.

5. Additional fees

Although payment for special items such as pasteups/graphics, intricate formatting, formulas and equations and "laundry lists" (lists of terms out of context) may be included in the section of price, there are other problematic areas that you may want to cover, such as handwritten or partially legible source text, obscure abbreviations or acronyms, slang or poetic style, or extensive research (assuming that the translator has not misrepresented his or her qualifications and the research required is indeed beyond that normal to routine translation procedure).

6. Additional costs

Who pays for overnight courier charges, long distance phone, modem and fax calls, extra copies, etc.?

7. Liability

Liability includes a wide variety of issues, such as:
What is the translator's liability for errors, either actual errors in a translation or lack of adherence to written instructions provided by the client?
If the client finds errors, will there be a reduction in pay? No pay?
Will the translator be liable for ensuing damages?
What is the statute of limitations on liability?
How will alleged errors be verified?

8. Confidentiality

A statement about keeping the source document and any support material confidential is important to protect the client, and serves to make the translator look more professional.

9. Property/copyright

Questions include:

Who owns the translation?
What about any glossaries compiled by the translator?
Can the translator retain file copies of the translation and original document, or must everything be returned to the client?

10. Changes by others

To protect the translator, it is a good idea to include a statement about not being responsible for the translation if it is reviewed and subsequently modified by others, which happens more often than not, either by editors and proofreaders contracted by the translation bureau or by a foreign representative or employee of the direct client. To protect your reputation, it might be a good idea to specify that if your translation is reviewed and changed by others, it must be returned to you for approval before it is used. Of course, then another issue arises, that of how to charge for the translator's time reviewing his or her edited translation, which can be very time-consuming in the case of large jobs and/or extensive changes.

11. Governing law

It is wise to specify that any disputes will be settled in the state where you live so you don't incur the expense of having to travel to the client's state in the unfortunate event of a lawsuit.

12. Merger clause

This is a provision stating that the written terms of your contract may not be modified by prior or oral agreement, and that any changes must be in writing and signed by both parties.

Other issues that you might want to consider, some of which I've seen in other contracts or which have been a problem for other translators, are as follows:

13. Responsibility for payment of workman's compensation, social security, local, state, and federal taxes.

Because of recent IRS cases, bureaus in particular usually include a clause saying that the contractor is responsible for payment of these taxes and insurance.

14. Subcontracting work to others

This too needs to be spelled out:
Is it allowed?
If not, what is the penalty for subcontracting to others?
What about extending confidentiality agreements to subcontractors?

15. Continuation clause

To avoid having to include many of the above terms in every agreement, which will be generic to every job, this clause would state that any future translation assignments will be covered by the same terms as specified in the "Blanket Agreement" until one party cancels. In this way, subsequent jobs can be governed by a shorter agreement that specifies the basic terms particular to the individual job, i.e., price, description, deadline, method and format of delivery.

In addition to having a written agreement, there are a few other recommended tips for ensuring satisfactory working relationships:

16. In your translation, be extremely careful with numbers, conversions, etc.

17. After you've finished, proofread your work line by line against the original text to make sure you haven't omitted anything.

18. Communicate with your client when you consider it advisable.

In this way you can discuss any troublesome or ambiguous passages or cultural problems noted in the text, so that you can agree on how to handle such problems. Don't assume anything until you've checked it out with the client.

19. Keep a "diary."

It is useful to keep a diary such as a Daytimer where you jot down written notes about the job you're working on, i.e., you called so and so on such and such a date to discuss XYZ problem, and this was the result of the discussion. In the event a question comes up after you've turned in the translation, you've got written documentation of what transpired.

The above issues cover a lot of potential trouble spots in any working relationship between a translator and a client, and not all may be needed in every agreement for every job. They have been presented to help translators think about areas that may apply to them, thereby avoiding misunderstandings and problems with clients and paving the way for a mutually beneficial and satisfying business relationship, one that is professional and honest and guided by integrity.

In Chinese, the character for "truth" is a person standing by his word. If we not only stand by our word, but get it in writing, we should be able to put an end to the vast majority of disagreements concerning the business aspects of translation and focus on what is emotionally and financially the most rewarding to us—translating.

TRANSLATION AGREEMENT

Date of this Agreement:

_____ of _____ ("Translator")
Translator's Name   Translator's Address

and

_____ of _____ ("Client")
Client's Name   Client's Address

hereby agree as follows:

1. <u>Description of services</u>. Translator, as an independent contractor, will provide the following service(s) [*Identify item(s) to be translated and the particular service(s) to be performed*]:

_____
_____
_____

Scheduled completion date is:

Translator shall make every effort to complete service(s) by the above date but shall not be responsible for delays in completion caused by events beyond Translator's control.

Method of delivery: _____

Format of delivery: _____

2. <u>Fee for services.</u> Client agrees to pay $ _____ as Translator's fee for the above service(s). Payment is due as follows:

_____
_____

The due dates for payment of fees and costs under this Agreement shall be the date(s) specified in this Agreement, provided that if no date is specified, the due date shall be the date of Translator's billing for the fees or costs. Any payments for fees or costs not received by Translator within ____ days of the due date will be deemed late and shall be subject to a ____ % per month late charge. Client agrees to be responsible for Translator's costs in collecting late payments due from Client, including reasonable attorneys' fees.

3. <u>Cancellation or withdrawal by Client</u>. If Client cancels or withdraws any portion of the item(s) described in paragraph 1 above prior to Translator's completion of the service(s), then, in consideration of Translator's

scheduling and/or performing said service(s) Client shall pay Translator the portion of the above fee represented by the percentage of total service(s) performed, but in any event not less than ___ % of said fee.

4. <u>Additional fees.</u> Additional fees will be payable, to be calculated as provided below, in the event the following additional services are required: (a) investigation, inquiry, or research beyond that normal to a routine translation is required because of ambiguities in the item(s) to be translated; (b) additional services are required because Client makes changes in the item(s) to be translated after the signing of this Agreement; and (c) Translator is requested to make changes in the translation after delivery of the translation, because of Client's preferences as to style or vocabulary, and such changes are not required for accuracy. Such additional fees will be calculated as follows:

_____

_____

5. <u>Additional costs.</u> Client shall reimburse Translator for necessary out-of-pocket expenses incurred by Translator that are not a normal part of routine translation procedure, such as overnight document delivery service requested by Client, long distance telephone and telefax expenses to clarify document ambiguity, etc.

6. <u>Client's review of translation.</u> Upon receipt of the translation from Translator, Client shall promptly review it, and within 30 days after receipt shall notify Translator of any requested corrections or changes. Translator shall correct, at no cost to Client, any errors made by Translator.

7. <u>Confidentiality.</u> All knowledge and information expressly identified by Client in writing as confidential which Translator acquires during the term of this Agreement regarding the business and products of Client shall be maintained in confidentiality by Translator and, except as expressly authorized by Client in writing, shall not be divulged or published by Translator and shall not be authorized by Translator to be divulged or published by others. Confidential information for purposes of this paragraph shall not include the following:

    a. Information which is or becomes available to the general public, provided the disclosure of such information did not result from a breach by Translator of this paragraph.

b. Terminological glossary entries compiled by Translator in the course of Translator's performance of the translation service(s) under this Agreement; provided, however, that Client and Translator may agree in writing that, upon payment by Client to Translator of an agreed-upon fee, such terminological glossary entries shall be the property of Client and shall be covered by the confidentiality provisions of this paragraph.

8. <u>Translation is property of client; copyright</u>. Upon Client's completion of all payments provided herein, the translation of the item(s) described in paragraph 1 above shall be the property of Client. Translator has no obligation to take any steps to protect any copyright, trademark or other right of Client with respect to the translation, except as may be expressly otherwise provided in this Agreement. Notwithstanding the foregoing, Translator shall have the right to retain file copies of the item(s) to be translated and of the translation, subject to the provisions of paragraph 7 above.

9. <u>Indemnification and hold-harmless by Client</u>. Client agrees to indemnify and hold Translator harmless from any and all losses, claims, damages, expenses or liabilities (including reasonable attorneys' fees) which Translator may incur based on information, representations, reports, data or product specifications furnished, prepared or approved by Client for use by Translator in the work performed under this Agreement.

10. <u>Changes by others.</u> Translator shall have no responsibility whatever as to any changes in the translation made by persons other than Translator.

11. <u>Governing law.</u> This Agreement shall be governed by the laws of the State of _____ .

12. Additional provisions. [*Add all additional provisions required by the parties.*]

_____
_____
_____
_____

13. Complete agreement. This is the complete agreement of the parties as to the subject matter hereof. Any changes in this Agreement must be in writing signed by both parties.

This Agreement becomes a binding contract only upon signature by both parties and the delivery of fully signed copies to each party.

Translator: _____

Client: _____

American Translators Association—Translation Agreement—July 1991 ed.

IMPORTANT NOTICE

THIS CONTRACT FORM OR GUIDE IS GENERAL IN NATURE AND IS NOT INTENDED TO PRESCRIBE THE USE OF ANY TERMS AND CONDITIONS HEREIN. THE ISSUANCE OF THIS FORM DOES NOT RESTRICT IN ANY RESPECT ANY MEMBER OR NON MEMBER FROM CONTRACTING FOR SERVICE ON TERMS AND CONDITIONS DIFFERENT FROM THOSE SET FORTH HEREIN. THE USE OF ANY PORTION OF THIS FORM OF AGREEMENT IS STRICTLY VOLUNTARY, AND IS THE SOLE RESPONSIBILITY OF THE CONTRACTING PARTIES.

NEITHER THE AMERICAN TRANSLATORS ASSOCIATION NOR ITS MEMBERS ASSUME ANY RESPONSIBILITY OR LIABILITY, WHETHER BASED ON WARRANTY, CONTRACT, NEGLIGENCE, STRICT LIABILITY, PRODUCT LIABILITY OR OTHERWISE, WITH RESPECT TO THE USE OF THIS CONTRACT FORM. THE AMERICAN TRANSLATORS ASSOCIATION AND ITS MEMBERS MAKE NO WARRANTY, EXPRESS OR IMPLIED, WITH REGARD TO THE LEGALITY OR ENFORCEABILITY OF THIS FORM OF AGREEMENT.

Section 2:

Challenges in a Global Economy

World Events Create Opportunities and Challenges for Translators and Interpreters: Translating Words Is But a Part

HELEN M. AND JOHN F. SZABLYA

In 1945 World War II came to an end. The first big showdown of war criminals at the Nuremberg Trials brought a tremendous need for simultaneous court interpreters. The acceleration went from consecutive to simultaneous, as interpreters became faster at doing a job which was at times so heartrending that interpreters had to leave their jobs after only a few weeks.

Recent world events have again created opportunities for hundreds of translators and interpreters as a result of the "velvet revolutions" that freed Central and Eastern Europe.

In 1945 the Soviets occupied most of that part of the world. By 1948 the Communist system ruled countries of the "Eastern Bloc" or, as many prefer to be called today, nations of Central Europe. With the collapse of the Communist system, a free-market economy is now opening up, and translators and interpreters are playing a key role in this development.

Western business, and as a result our profession, is faced with an enormous demand, convertible into a market of the same size, ready to absorb the world's products and services, while supplying it with many of its own. This demand/market convertibility often depends on countries with free market economies. Newly liberated countries need our experience and technology in a non-threatening way. Money reinvested into the economy for lucrative returns will also provide the work force in those countries with the income necessary to buy our products and services.

Europe has opened up in the past two years. A wise manufacturer or consulting firm with long-range possibilities in mind can open a factory/office in the custom-free zones in Hungary, and be less than 100 miles away from Europe's lucrative market, as well as from the dormant potential of Eastern European countries, including Russia.

Among would-be investors and their Central or Eastern European counterparts there is tremendous confusion. Neither can understand what the other wants, or needs, in terms of information, even if both speak the same language, e.g., English. This communication gap can be overcome only by people well versed in two systems. One, in which the new Central and Eastern European entrepreneurs were brought up and the other, the American/Western way of thinking. It becomes obvious that translating words is important but far from enough.

The need to fill this gap prompted several translators/interpreters with business backgrounds and connections in their respective countries, to branch into trade consulting. Our company was one of these.

When we write about our own experiences, we do not mean that each and every translator/interpreter has to have the same education and/or professional experience in order to do trade consulting. To the contrary: we want to point out that any experience can be used in connection with translation and interpretation. Take what you have and convert it into a money-making proposition.

A Case Study

Some concepts that exist in one way of thinking do not exist in the other way, while others have to be explained and renamed, as those concepts have changed throughout the 40 years when planned economies were cut off from, and were conditioned to be antagonistic towards, free market ideas. Often the language of emigrés and those who remained in the old country developed in such different directions that they became completely foreign to each other.

Our own background in Marxist and American business practices gives us a great advantage when it comes to translating not only words, but ways of thinking. Often two people talk the same language, yet it is impossible for them to understand each other because a certain word means a different concept for each of them.

An American and a Ukrainian businessman met in Budapest, Hungary. They were discussing the advantages of a free market economy as related to their new joint venture. The Ukrainian declared: "Finally, we will be able to get rid of our worst enemy, the middleman." The American businessman, aware of the total lack of a distribution system, paled as he retorted: "But it is exactly what you need, a middleman!"

Had they been alone, this would have been the end of a promising business relationship, a joint venture. Luckily, a trade consultant, well versed in both "ways of thinking," knew that one was talking about black marketeers, and the other about distributors. She straightened them out. They learned that their ideas about business were the same, but their terminology was not.

Although the present article deals with our personal experiences as related to Hungary, we believe that almost all professional translators and interpreters could apply the concepts presented to their own benefit, adapted specifically to their geographic areas of interest.

Why Translators Can Add an Extra Dimension

Many of the professional translators in the U.S. were born in other countries and many others have studied abroad. Our case is no exception.

When growing up in Hungary, John learned several languages. As a child, he was part of a family that alternated among four languages, designating only one for any given day of the week. Learning several languages was very customary in Hungary because the Hungarian language is not used widely outside of that country and we were expected to understand and speak other languages when it came to the world market. Earning several university degrees after World War II, John became an associate professor at the Technical University of Budapest. He was required to study thousands of pages of Marxism in order to be able to answer students' questions, in case he was asked. Although he is an electrical engineer, his PhD is in economics. All of this gave him an in-depth knowledge of the system which today is undergoing such rapid change.

Helen was brought up to lead her family business in Hungary, consisting of a chain of drugstores, and the wholesale and manufacture of drugstore-related commodities (excluding pharmaceuticals). She acted as simultaneous interpreter for her father in his business negotiations as early as the age of 14. The Communists, of course, took their business, but she remained interested in business and languages. The Marxists also nationalized her school when she was 14, so that from that age she had to study three hours of Marxism a day. She, like her husband, knows intimately how Marxists think. She can interpret not only the language, but also the ideology and culture, in only a few words or sentences when she works with business people. That is why she decided to expand her translation business into trade consulting.

The Szablyas left Hungary in 1956, which is a story in itself. Since that time they have been actively involved in academic and business communities. Helen started an import business (mainly books) in Canada shortly after their arrival there. She also continued her education in business at the University of British Columbia. This, and her continuous business efforts at selling and publicizing her writing, translating and lecturing, kept her up-to-date with American business.

Both of the authors have been very involved with the latest developments in Hungary. John joined Helen in her business following his retirement. As trade consultants, the authors use all of their knowledge and experience to translate ways of thinking and give realistic business advice under present circumstances.

A Bit of Marxist Background

Dealing with Central European countries, especially Hungary, which served as the testing ground for *glasnost* starting in 1972, is completely different than dealing with the countries of the former Soviet Union. In Central European countries many remember the free market system and the workings of democracy. In the former Soviet Union, even if there were people old enough to remember pre-World War I times, they never had a free market system under the czars.

Just what are the crucial characteristics of this different way of thinking that is to be translated over and over?

Marxist-educated people had their own peculiar "freedoms":

1. Freedom from financial concerns from cradle to grave

Everything was paid for from the minute they were born. However, whoever paid their bill, in this case the Communist State, also decided on what it was going to pay for. They had no choice in what they were receiving, as it was free.

2. Freedom from decision-making.

No grassroots approach existed. Decisions were made at the top. An individual could only grumble about the laws and regulations. Everything—good or bad—came down from the State.

This caused people in planned economies to become used to living without *choice*. Naturally, if you have no *choice*, you cannot be held *responsible* either. No one wants to be responsible for anything to the extreme that they shy away from advertising, publicity and promotion. All such activities by an individual used to be considered aggression against the state, as no private individual was allowed to get engaged in entrepreneurial activities.

Advertising was out of the question. Who in his right mind would want to make public that he or she is involved in illegal activities?

Other business concepts were also unknown, for example marketing. Marketing implies that you focus your efforts on something. Yet, in formerly Marxist countries diversification was a must. For example, if, according to a new rule, duplicating were outlawed, but you also had a translating agency, you were still in business. If you specialized in copying, you were finished.

Overhead and cost-accounting are still equally foreign. For example, the president of a large bank told me, "I don't understand these Americans. What do they want from us? We always have to fill out all those papers and then they don't pay. Why work for nothing?" He simply did not understand the concept that no one pays for the proposals, bids, loan applications; that these are "overhead" costs and risks you have to take. You recover them in your unit price, hourly fees, and/or commission.

Simple concepts that grade school children learned in Hungary before World War II, such as draft, check, mortgage, and escrow had to be explained to managers of companies after the velvet revolution.

Pricing was a political issue in planned economies and had nothing to do with the fluctuation of supply and demand. Now they have to take the jolts of reality as they plunge into the free market and deregulated prices.

Implications for Translators

To explain and solve these problems is the job of a trade consultant, who may well be an interpreter or translator, with intimate knowledge of both situations and with a true desire to help.

Although our case study is taken from Central Europe at a given historic moment, the principles demonstrated in this article can be applied to any country, or cultural entity, and in any period of history. Every business manager or researcher in any given discipline can benefit from the expertise of native consultants or experts who intimately know their market.

Our United States-based marketing efforts should concentrate on developing and promoting the concept of "owner's translator/interpreter," based on the precedent of "owner's engineer." The latter has been widely used in the construction industry for ages. He or she overlooks the projects and makes certain that everything is done to specification, and works as it should in the end.

All business people need someone on their side whom they can trust to provide them with the true meaning of the written or pronounced concepts in case of an important translation. For example: We have seen a joint venture proposal that had been translated by someone in a foreign country. The English text specified all mentioned currencies as non-convertible, while the foreign language text spoke of convertible currencies. A "tiny" translation error such as this can mean a sizable loss to someone. We highly recommend to every one of our clients: even if the translation is done in another country, an "owner's translator/ interpreter" should review the finished product/contract before any binding, or potentially binding papers are signed.

Public Relations Then

As told earlier, decades of Communist rule led to ways of thinking in Central and Eastern Europe unlike those in the West. Advertising, public relations, and similar activities were implicitly forbidden. There were two reasons for this attitude: the first one originated in Marxist ideology; and the second in the omnipotent control of the state over the individual.

According to Marxist ideology with its planned economy, advertising was not needed. The state decided (planned) what goods should be produced, in what quantities, and at what price they should be sold. Consequently, there was no need to advertise. Advertising is needed if a source of a good or goods (including services and other products) wants to persuade the public that its product has certain advantages over that offered by another source(s), whether it be an advantage in price, convenience, quality or something else. If there is only one source, one quality, and one price, why advertise at all?

In addition, Marx believed that advertising was an invention of the "dirty capitalists" which just increased the cost of goods, its sole purpose being to sell to the public poor quality products. One has to keep in mind that Marx developed his theories in the second half of the nineteenth century, when conditions were very different from those of today. Also, cheap energy was not yet available to ease the burden of the physical laborer, or, in other terms, of the working class. As a matter of fact, Marx died in 1883, just when electricity was first being introduced.

However, it was not just Marxism, and the consequential harsh political system, which made advertising, public relations, etc. nonexistent. Since the sole producer was the state, individuals were harshly punished if caught doing anything even closely resembling private enterprise.

No one in his or her right mind wants to advertise activities which would result in stiff jail sentences. No wonder advertising and public relations were unknown to people living in the Eastern Bloc.

Public Relations Now

The so called Iron Curtain is gone, and all the news sources tell us that big changes are taking place in Central and Eastern Europe. Big changes indeed. We, here in the U.S., are upset if our government changes a few rules. Imagine if the entire basis of daily life were to change. This is exactly what is happening in Central and Eastern Europe. The centrally planned economy is being replaced by free market forces.

In the new free market economy the former Eastern Bloc countries need to learn to look at advertising as an investment. It is not an expense that needs to be squeezed out of what is left over after everything else is paid. It must be considered up front, and, as a result, if applied properly, it will bring great dividends.

People of the Central and Eastern European countries, and, as a matter of fact, other countries moving from a centrally planned economy into a free market era, learn fast. Still, to unlearn, and then learn new things after many years of indoctrination is not an easy task, and it takes a long time. It could take as long as a generation.

Yet, the concept of public relations is becoming evident. For example, the January 1992 issue of the *Public Relations Journal* talked about a special conference seminar where representatives from newly established Hungarian, Soviet and Polish public relations associations talked about how public relations, hitherto unknown in these countries, can really work and assist businesses in their respective homelands.

The Future

Translation tends to be more expensive in the United States than in some other parts of the world. Again, with the help of public relations we can explain why business people need good translators. If a sizable project is translated in another country, especially if it is done by the foreign business partner of a project, or deal, we strongly recommend that the American business partner(s) hire(s) an *"owner's translator."*

Although applicable to any country, American business people negotiating with counterparts from the Central and Eastern European countries face exceptionally difficult times. Cultural differences can enter the picture even in the smallest ways. For example, smoking is still a symbol of relaxation in many places in Europe. The color associated with little girls in this country is the color for little boys in France. Smoothing over such differences or preparing the businessman can be part of the task of the translator or interpreter.

The "owner's translator" should thus have many tasks to perform. Probably the most important is to read through all documents, making sure the translation is accurate. The amount charged by the translator is a small sum to pay in order to avoid costly mistakes. For example, a "small" error of three or more zeros in a contract, which may come about by not distinguishing between the American and certain European countries' interpretation of the words "billion," "trillion," and so forth, will spell disaster later.

Public relations will show the client that advertising in foreign countries can be quite tricky. The meaning and the spirit of the advertisement, not merely the words have to be translated into a different culture. One good solution is to contact a U.S. trade consultant or translator. The best translations come from cooperation between e.g., an American-Hungarian translator and an English-speaking Hungarian translator, advertising agency, and/or professional. Such a combination will capture the spirit of the advertisement and translate that into the same spirit expressed in the Hungarian culture.

Public Relations Help the Translator

If public relations can help the people of Central and Eastern Europe, imagine how much more it can help us translators. Our objective is to sell translation/interpretation services to clients. Therefore, we have to relate equally well to our clients, our employers, our co-workers or colleagues, and our employees. Every one of these relationships is crucial for our company's well-being.

Simple steps like these, adapted from a State of Maryland circular, when dealing with clients, or potential clients:

- Listen to everything they have to say.
- Sort out in your mind what the clients really want.
- Respond to people, not the organization.
- Listen to their hearts as well as their words.
- Deal with their problem, not yours.
- If you can't help, can someone else?
- If no one can help, at least show that you care and convey your conclusion honestly.

As translators and interpreters, we can promote public relations and our profession in other specific ways:

1. Forming links with colleagues

Meet with colleagues, such as at meetings of local translator and interpreter associations, and forge valuable links with them. Organize events, or participate in groups that organize such events and help in a noticeable way. Soon you will have referrals from fellow translators and interpreters who will appreciate your public relations and your willingness to help.

2. Finding your target audience

Finding clients and convincing them you are the person for the job is of course essential. At the same time, you can focus on target groups to which you want to become visible. Consider where you can get to those whose interest you want to catch.

3. Promoting ourselves.

This can be extremely difficult for introverted translators who would rather die than brag. Yet, in today's market brag we must if we are to succeed. You have to show you are the expert. In the cover letter you should mention your credentials, the best and most important translations you have done. Include letters of appreciation from clients; the more important, the better. Once you have found your target audience, explain to them WHY YOU should be the one doing their translation. Research your individual targets, know their interests and address them separately, matching your own qualifications.

4. Giving thought to presentation

Presentation is very important. Acquire a good, easy-to-use desk publishing program. Good design and color will make your projects get noticed. Color copying is not overly expensive any more. Remember that marketing or packaging does not replace good work and valuable content.

5. Promoting our profession

Public relations also includes the promotion, marketing of your product or service in particular, as well as general public relations regarding our profession. The translator's work is to make the client's work easy. The right public relations explains to clients about translators and how they can find the best one for their purposes, also how they can make the translator's work easier.

6. Keeping the client informed

Our interpersonal relationships may determine whether the next job will come our way, or someone else's way instead. Furthermore, since as translators we bridge cultures, we must try to keep our client informed. Notes on cultural differences, explanations of nuances and tiny shades of meanings are usually appreciated.

7. Showing appreciation of others

Another part of our good will or a type of public relations is to show appreciation of others. If you consult experts in the field in the course of doing a translation, it is a good idea to add their name (and therefore, prestige) to your translation.

Conclusion

We as translators have a new opportunity well worth exploring in cooperation with translators and translation agencies in foreign countries. We should pool our expertise with colleagues in the respective countries by building up our connections and setting up joint translating/interpreting ventures with them.

Services translators/interpreters can offer include: finding matches for businesses using our old and new connections; specialized translation/interpretation; marketing and promotion; publicity and advertising; help with relocation, including housing and amenities for families; locating real estate for business. Opportunities are endless.

All the above hold, particularly when the translation or interpretation involves a language from one of the Central or Eastern European Countries, or of any other country in transition.

Translators, and interpreters have great opportunities if they just take advantage of their intimate knowledge of the culture and ways of thinking of another nation, and use the right kind of public relations and advertising to promote and market themselves.

A characteristic of intelligent people is to look for new ideas and implement them. Translators and interpreters should look for new opportunities based on their past, their background and ethnic expertise, and make good use of them. The North American business community will need all the expertise it can get in order to conquer world markets in the next millennium.

Translation and International Trade

DORIS GANSER

"We, the people doing international business, are the ones bringing the world together, not the diplomats," stated E. David Seals, president of AMC Entertainment International, at a presentation. "But most can't do it without translators and interpreters," we might add, "because we are the facilitators who allow them to communicate with each other."

International business in the United States would not be able to function efficiently, were it not for the assistance rendered by those who translate and interpret, but especially by translators to languages other than English. "It is my honest belief that at least 30% of our foreign trade deficit would disappear if American business could learn how to effectively utilize foreign languages and professional translators and interpreters and would employ experts who are thoroughly familiar with the structure and culture of other countries, particularly the culture of doing business," writes Harry Obst in *The Polyglot*, Winter 1992.

Yet many in international trade are still barely beginning to understand that one cannot pick up a barmaid or governess fresh off the boat and use her as a translator; that linguists may know all about a language and perhaps speak it well enough to convey their own thoughts, but that translators and interpreters must have the ability to communicate thoughts between two often greatly distinct parties, i.e., they must convey the thoughts of others; and that good professional translators must have qualities far beyond: they have to convey the concepts and ideas the originator created and adapt them to exact situations and cultures. In conveying the thoughts of others, they must find a way of reaching an audience that is both generic and specific.

National and local associations of translators strive to make translation users, including international traders, better aware of the need to employ professional translators to obtain professional translations. But we have only defined in rather general terms who we are, what qualifications and knowledge such professionals should have and what is required of them, especially in the relationship with international business where success in the marketplace is greatly affected by the background of the translator who is involved in the "deal."

We have always concentrated on the process of arriving at a good translation (by whatever definition) and the knowledge required for it in the technical aspect but not sufficiently on the consultant role of the translator and on the ultimate purpose of the translation. Based on hundreds of résumés read by the author, asking for a statement about translation, translators and those who would like to be translators have again and again indicated that they are or would like to be translators because they conceive of it as something interesting, even romantic, because they "love foreign languages," and similar. Very few, if any, have stated clearly that they are interested in international business, that they would like to contribute to the balance of trade, and none have mentioned the ultimate purpose of translation, although some statements have referred to "keeping the audience in mind."

Even though we have specified that translators must be familiar with the subject area, we have failed to make most translators specifically aware of what business needs—that to do good and useful translations for international trade, one should have a thorough understanding of its workings and intricacies, not just the "subject" and words from a dictionary. Because of their background—one-track linguistic or other specialized education at a university but frequently a lack of interdisciplinary or translator training and above all of practical experience in business, many translators have never actually witnessed an international business transaction from A to Z. Translations are produced with some vaguely assumed audience in mind, not with the multiple diverse targets that exist in world markets. Many U.S. translators to English have the privilege of specializing. Because of the diversity of business transactions even within one and the same company, this advantage is usually not available to those cooperating closely with their partners in international trade who have to provide translations for a multitude of situations, whether they are working in-house or as freelances. Working with agencies instead of individual translators may alleviate the problem for business in some cases, provided the agency uses translators and/or revisors-editors who understand global trading.

To illustrate this claim, let us view a typical Tender or Invitation to Bid from a Latin American country to an interested American company which purchased the tender documents.

After flipping through a 100-page or thicker "legal" document with, according to the customer, a few financial and general technical terms, specialized legal translator Joe Lex accepts the assignment of a Spanish to English translation in good faith, albeit with an extremely short deadline—the latter just about the only thing of which the client was clearly apprised by his Latin American representative. For clarification: potential bidders almost always receive the bidding documents "at the last moment." It is generally not the translator's customer who arbitrarily delays and then sets unreasonable deadlines but the customer's need to meet a bidding deadline set by a foreign agency or government; it may, in fact, be from a country in which holidays do not coincide with those in the United States.

One very advantageous way of cooperating closely with the customer consists in reading the document thoroughly from beginning to end, noting and immediately notifying the customer of urgent or past deadlines, exceptional conditions or payment terms, bonds and insurance, anything that's not boilerplate. Above all, based on the technical conditions, the translator should review the goods and services to be supplied. If the Invitation to Bid is for products other than those the customer ordinarily supplies—and that's not unusual—the customer should be immediately advised even though it will most likely mean that he is no longer interested in the translation but will happily pay well for the reading time (and come back another day). To do so requires understanding how international bidding works. For the sake of simplicity, we shall assume here that the customer can, indeed, supply the goods and services requested in the Invitation.

Joe Lex, unfamiliar with international business, flips through the job, starts translating and finds the beginning 35 or so pages to consist of the legal requirements, although containing "non-standard" terminology, Spanglish or a mixture of both (occasionally even proper Spanish) which he discovers later to be the type of language prevailing in the entire document. When Joe encounters an unclear, perhaps erroneous term, he adds "sic" and goes on. He faithfully marks that a paragraph or two appear to be missing, points out that the bottoms of several pages are practically illegible, thoroughly translates that a confirmation of receipt of the document is required the next day ... he is making good progress, his translation is quite correct, and he has four more days to complete his work.

Yet a major mistake has occurred: the client has just failed to meet an important deadline because Joe did not immediately advise of the confirmation requirement, thinking "it has nothing to do with translating." By missing this first deadline, the client may or may not be allowed to bid (although exceptions are granted but must be specifically requested). If no exception is granted after the translation is delivered, the translation has become useless to the customer, since only bidders who have appropriately sent their confirmation will be permitted to enter bids, according to the document.

Joe Lex should have also made every attempt and taken extra time to determine as much as possible of the contents of practically illegible portions, instead of just noting the fact and grumbling, and if impossible, he should have made the customer—again immediately—aware of the illegibility of certain portions, the missing paragraph, the unclear word so that, depending on the situation, clarifications and/or more legible copy could have been obtained by the time the bulk of the translation was delivered—the moment at which the customers's painstaking work of preparing the bid can finally begin. These are situations in which translators must work hand in hand with their customers who cannot know what deadlines or difficulties might be encountered because they can't read what they receive in a foreign language.

Legal bid conditions list, among other information, certain documents which must accompany the U.S. company's bid. An alert translator can advise an inexperienced or first time international bidder of those listed requirements which involve lengthy bureaucratic processes, e.g., a notarized Certificate of Incorporation in Spanish, a Certificate of Appointment of a Latin American (Country) Official Representative for the purposes of the bid in question, etc.; these are papers which, after having been translated to a foreign language, must be routed via specific state, federal and/or foreign offices before being allowed to enter into foreign legal channels. The customer can initiate translation to the foreign language and take other action regarding administrative and legal matters while awaiting the translation to English. This will permit the customer's technical and engineering staff to concentrate on preparing the technical bid later—but only if the translator notifies him promptly.

Gradually, Joe Lex works himself through the financial conditions which are part of every international bidding document. They state certain bonds and/or insurance expected from every bidder, their validity period as well as the conditions of payment imposed upon the successful bidder (unless the company succeeds in negotiating concessions in advance). Needless to say, here is another point where the customer can undertake advance work, if advised by the translator early enough.

The financial portion normally also lists penalties for not signing the contract after having been declared the successful bidder and for non-compliance with any of the conditions of the ensuing contract after signing. Misused terms, such as, perhaps "initiation guarantee" (instead of "bid bond" or several standard equivalents) or "fob" without a place of delivery or point of transfer of risk are discrepancies the customer will generally be able to catch in the translated copy but it does not hurt to mention them early on. After receiving the translation, the customer will be feverishly busy in an effort to complete his bid, and so every little bit of early help the translator can provide to facilitate the customer's job will be a plus (whether the customer ever realizes it or not ... most don't, but professionals do the job well, no matter what).

The financial terms may also include a formula related to the conditions of payment and/or penalties. Joe Lex neatly cuts out or scans the original formula into his translated copy. But these formulas are generally not transparent without explanations of the abbreviations used. Professional translator Joe Lex just omitted doing so.

Specialized legal translator Joe is now in for a shock. All along, there had been a few interspersed technical terms, as he had been advised, and he was able to find most of them in his dictionaries. What follows are detailed technical specifications. Had he known what parts a standard bidding document comprises, he would have anticipated and thoroughly reviewed this portion of the documentation and realized the great versatility required of anyone translating the entire set of documents. By now, it is Day 4, and not much time left to tell the client he is not versed in aviation, avionics and electronics, the subject areas involved. He really does not feel competent to tackle the task, especially since he can find few of the terms in the technical dictionaries at the library, but he plugs along ... he promised to deliver on time. The result is inadequate. The client has to waste time and money to consult with his Latin American representative and others, yet is still not 100% sure of all the details.

Translators working for firms involved in international bidding only rarely have a chance to pick and choose parts of a job they accept. They must have a good understanding of the entire transaction, legal, financial, and technical/scientific implications and the ability to work on such material under extreme time pressure, without much time to dig in reference works, even in the initial translations to English similar to Joe Lex's job.

Occasionally, a more experienced client will ask for an annotated advance copy of the bidding documents or perhaps request the technical portion (or just forms) to be completed before the remainder of the translation is done, so that the in-house engineering, financial or legal staffs can begin preparing some of the many documents which must be submitted in conjunction with bids. In other cases, a draft will be requested for delivery with "the speed of lightning," i.e., the translator is given even less time for a pound or two of documents, then another day or so for revisions. In this case, when delivering the final copy, it is very useful to enclose the draft translation copy with hand corrections, in addition to the final revised copy. Thus, the client need not reread the entire document but can simply scan areas with changes to determine whether they have any significant effect on the ultimate bid submitted. In yet another situation, the translator may be consulted by the client to determine which portions should be translated, should be translated first, etc. The translator must understand the intricacies of such projects to assist in the selection process.

Even when an agency (instead of an individual translator) is requested to arrange for the translations, there is seldom enough time to prepare glossaries of terminology which would allow several translators to be used (provided they don't ignore the glossaries, no matter how many times requested to use them). The agency, therefore, prefers a single highly versatile translator for all the terms and conditions, instead of dividing the job up, or else different terminology will appear in different portions of the document with insufficient time left to have an editor pull all of it together. Glossaries, even for relatively transparent terms, are extremely useful because most of the bids have to be submitted in the foreign language. A translator or a crew of translators to the foreign language must often begin working on the bid translation, even before the entire translation to English is completed. Client-changes while translating bids to a foreign language are common-place and require great attention to detail and original terminology as well as flexibility on the part of the translator. Even though the terminology in the Invitation may be non-standard, Spanglish, or even wrong, the actual bid must contain the same terminology as the Invitation or may be considered not to be in conformance with the bid specifications. If the original Spanish document contained *"caseta"* which was correctly translated to English as "shelter" (for the equipment), then it is simply not acceptable to translate "shelter" back to Spanish by "*abrigo*," etc., even though correct in another context.

The translator to the foreign language is provided or should request the original Invitation in the foreign language, because it is in the client's best interest that the original terminology be used. Many translators violently oppose such concessions and insist on using their own "correct" terminology. Yet the "correct" terminology may reduce their client's chances of receiving the contract award, unless he has filed exceptions to certain terminology in advance (in the case of exceptions, they are taken under advisement by the Contract Award Committee in the foreign country, and if approved, all bidders are advised of these and other bidders' approved changes, usually with a specific cut-off date stated in the Invitation, a date after which no exceptions and changes can be requested). In other words, the "perfect" translation may lose the customer the deal. Many customers are not even aware of these requirements so that in-house translators may cause the same problems as freelances and translation bureaus whose revisors or editors tend to remove "wrong" terminology. (If translators are concerned about their reputation when using "inappropriate" terminology, there is always the possibility to include an exception statement explaining discrepancies or disagreements on a separate page for the client's attention.)

Similar attention to discrepancies is required in the translation to English of a Letter of Credit. If it contains typos or spelling errors, strange terminology, etc., they should be pointed out to the customer so he can request a change to the L/C, because "correctly" back-translating a foreign language misnomer in invoices, bills of lading, etc. can invalidate the L/C and prevent timely payment upon shipment. If no change to the L/C is requested or received, it is advisable to retain misspelled words in all documentation, e.g., if the Spanish copy reads "caf" instead of "cif," the documents should pick up "delivery caf" (Mexico City etc.) and not cif; a parenthesis with the correct INCO term is occasionally a last way out of the dilemma.

International bids and letters of credit are only some of the areas which require close cooperation between translator and client in international trade. If copy in English is badly written, direct consultation with the customer is the best method because some customers may be able to express themselves more clearly verbally than in written form.

Translators to languages other than English who have been able to function in the international business environment have, for many years, felt somewhat uncomfortable about a certain lack of understanding of their "differentness" encountered even from fellow-translators working to English. These colleagues know about different types of translation, those for information and those for publication, and about different rules that might apply to each; that a good translation must be audience-oriented; that the translator must understand the subject areas involved in a particular job, and much more. But the discomfort, a feeling of almost being in a different profession, continued. Eventually translators of some languages banded together in language-specific groups. The ATA's division movement (presently there are Portuguese, Russian and Japanese divisions) initially originated to a great extent from translators to a foreign language who felt that speaking and translating **to** the same language united them by similar objectives, interests, and problems which they considered to be unique to their language. Because most translate to a single foreign language, they did not realize that the trend toward division was probably not only related to their specific language but to another major underlying cause, namely the fact that all translators to a foreign language—generally for international business, its advertising agencies, attorneys and/or accountants—are doing work which is often quite different from translations to English. Perhaps translators to foreign languages should have jointly united in a single division or interest group because their common activity distinguishes them and causes them to be faced with many like aspects of their activity as a binding element, no matter to what language they translate.

1. The type of material translated often differs

Only a small portion of the material translated to foreign languages for international business is intended for information; much of it is for publication and will, therefore, be **directly** disseminated to a much larger public than most translation to English; and mistakes may be immediately multiplied 100,000 or more times. This applies particularly to consumer and technical advertising, videos shown at expos, training films, movies, labels on drugs, pesticides and potentially poisonous chemicals. Such work requires unusual attention to cultural adaptation and may involve translator-initiated changes in products, colors, pictures and, in the case of conversions, even reviews to determine whether the curves are still applicable after conversion. Sometimes the translated copy (or at least a glossary) can be sent overseas for review although direct contact with the U.S. company's overseas agent to clarify points or terminology is often more useful to the translator and sometimes permitted by the customer (and **not** permitted without the U.S. customer's approval).

2. The method of translating differs

The age-old adage that "translation should be as literal as possible and as free as necessary" continues to stand and apply to all areas of the profession. The only true secret of a good translator is the knowledge about where the dividing line between literal and free translation should fall in each case. It sounds simple enough but takes years, perhaps decades, to learn how to arrive at a translation that "reads as if an educated author had written it in his or her own language" (which may have been first stated so appropriately by Patricia Newman). Or, according to Harry Obst in *The Polyglot*, Winter 1992, "the litmus test for professional translations is very simple. If you have never seen the original and you recognize that you are looking at a translation, it is not a good translation. You need to be told that it is a translation."

Different schools of thought have prevailed over the years. Many translators claim that it is perfectly all right to say "what I see is what you, the client, get; it's not my job to adapt your inappropriate copy." Their results cannot possibly meet the requirements stated above and are not suitable in the international business environment (and probably not elsewhere). They neglect the fact that translation has a purpose.

The latest buzzwords are "globalization," "localization," and "internationalization" (and probably several others) which have been surfacing in the advertising of many firms, including translation companies. Good translators and a fair number of translation companies have always "globalized" their translations, while others delivered their customers "just" translations and now have a ready-made excuse: If customers complain because their overseas contacts happen to discover some inadequate rendering of an image or phrase, they say that they had not been asked for a "globalized" translation (overheard in a session on globalization at the 1992 ATA Conference in San Diego).

Every translation to a foreign language should be and should, in the past, have been globalized, localized, internationalized; it is now becoming clear that this has not always been the case. Herein lies one of the causes of the uneasiness many translators to foreign languages have felt over the years. Those who had been "globalizing" (without the buzzword) had been competing with Translators or Companies X, Y, and Z who offered the same translations faster and at considerably lower rates (information obtained from customers not from fellow-translators or competing agencies), while they themselves had been putting many additional ingredients into their good translation mix; they had not known that in making the cake, some others had always left out "eggs, butter and spices," and all the client could see was the "beautiful sugar frosting."

Everyone combines the ingredients of a good translation in a different manner, even though each translator has knowledge of the basic ingredients of the cake. The secret of the superb chef/translator and to really good, truly "globalized," "internationalized" or "localized" translations lies simply in a few extra ingredients which add the "spice" to the cake, and it is about how much of each of the ingredients must go in, how to mix them appropriately together, when the opportune moment is for the addition of one of the ingredients and which one to omit in one situation or another. Let's hope that more translators actually begin to understand, now that we have buzzwords for this type of activity. No one has ever measured the impact sugar-frosted cardboard cakes have had on the U.S. balance of trade.

3. The audience is varied, unclearly defined and situated in a non-uniform, often fragmented market

Commercial and technical translation, the type required in international trade at all levels, has a distinct purpose but varying audience. Translations of advertising and brochures must help market a product or service overseas, foreign language versions of manuals, such as operating instructions for mechanical, electrical, electronic and computer equipment or software, must allow an operator to run the equipment.

Overseas users of such manuals may have greatly divergent levels of education, from ill-educated to highly sophisticated, and in some cases, the translator must find a happy medium to address all of them. Training manuals for technical or scientific equipment must allow the trainers from a foreign country to teach their firm's employees how to use machinery, instruments, and devices; while the trainer may be highly educated, the employee may be at a much lower educational level. The translator should not rely on the U.S. exporter or manufacturer to adapt a manual written for U.S. markets and levels of education properly to match the overseas audience or on a foreign trainer's ability to modify the language while giving a presentation and even less on the ability of an interpreter during a presentation to adapt the language. Finding the right level and tone requires sensitivity and research as well as early discussion and close cooperation between customer and translator. No matter what our wish list as translators may be, our clients are only human, and humans are simply not ideal. So we must put up with them (if they were perfect, they would not need us), work with them, and help them as much as we can. And while doing so, we can instill in them quite a bit of respect for our profession. Most of them are happy to cooperate when they realize that we are educated enough to understand their business and that by cooperating with us, we can help them better achieve **their** goals: more overseas sales, better training for their overseas clients, a better image for them and their overseas customer in the marketplace, prevention of legal problems, thus more money in their bank accounts—that, in turn, keeps us in business.

When a customer cannot afford different copy and printing for each individual market, translated copy must be suitable to address different types of customers in different countries, without offending anyone. Many times, one and the same copy must be carefully reviewed to make it suitable for all Spanish-speaking countries, including the U.S. market, or all German-speakers.

4. In translating to foreign languages, the translator's degree of responsibility is much greater

When an international engineering firm bids on a million-dollar project, translation errors, omissions, or other discrepancies (as described above) may cost the firm a large job. The client's financial stake may be immense—even the cost of simply preparing a bid is enormous. The translator's responsibility increases, as the size or value of the project bid rises.

If expensive four-color advertising in a foreign language does not hit home, the consumer will not buy. Since inadequate (not necessarily wrong) advertising translation can cause the lack of effectiveness of an advertisement or an entire advertising campaign, the translator to a foreign language must carefully weigh every word, every slogan before accepting it. And yet often, while ad or campaign materials are meticulously planned, submitted and resubmitted, preapproved, discussed, rejected, reapproved, negotiated, and finally approved in a cooperative effort between advertising company and client, a single translator or bureau (involving a translator and an editor/revisor or two) has sole responsibility for the end result in a foreign language—what they deliver gets printed, aired....

Improperly translated operating manuals with which the translator's customer cannot get the machine working, may not only lose him his overseas client but he may incur stiff penalties. With inadequate translations of technical training manuals, the training may be entirely wasted.

In lawsuits or patent litigation, the translator bears immense responsibility when an overseas company provides wrong information during the discovery phase of a lawsuit in response to a mistranslated question. A company overseas may completely underestimate the significance of a summons and its required response upon service abroad in accordance with The Hague Convention, if terms such as "summons" or "complaint" are translated to non-legal German terminology, instead of being presented in proper terms.

In the translation of drug labels and other medical and scientific material from U.S. firms or hospitals, the life and welfare of humans may be at stake. While there has been an increasing degree of outside verification (overseas) of this type of foreign language material over the decades, much responsibility continues to repose in the translator.

5. Smaller number of translators—greater versatility needed

As mentioned regarding bidding documents, the work of certain customers inherently requires translators with great versatility, whether to English or to a foreign language.

In order to meet the criteria of good translations, they should be done by professional translators from the target language country. Logically, in the United States, the selection of professional "native" translators to a foreign language is much smaller than that of translators to English. Because of their smaller numbers, most of them must be very versatile and be able to handle many different subjects and types of material.

While for translations to most major languages, the Translation Services Directories published by local and national translator associations may contain several translators specializing in different subject areas, certain languages have only a few persons listed who must obviously handle numerous subject matters, and many are perfectly capable of doing so.

For other languages, such as Sinhalese, for which such directories probably do not list a single translator, the problem of finding one cannot be easily solved. When one is discovered after a proverbial search like for a needle in a haystack, the translation agency or client cannot be too choosy and must sometimes use numerous editors to arrive at an acceptable translation.

But why use translators in the United States, when surely there are considerably more educated speakers/translators of, e.g., Sinhalese in Sri

Lanka, than in this country? The understanding of English of those available in the foreign country may be inadequate; this still leaves the problem of finding a translator or even speaker of the language with the right subject area specialization. If the subject area editor does not know English, an interpreter may be required to explain to him or her the finer points of copy content. Moreover, there may be equipment inadequacies so that, for many reasons, jobs have to be rejected several times before becoming even marginally acceptable. That's aside from different concepts regarding deadlines which may also cause difficulties.

The more translations in different subject areas a translator does, the better (s)he generally (and hopefully) becomes in translating, especially with feedback from the direct client or translation agency. Many translation agencies have learned to juggle between persons (translators and non-translator consultants) in both countries who cooperate on one and the same job, negotiating, coaching, explaining (both verbally and in writing), verifying and reverifying to ultimately arrive at a good translation. All this usually happens under time pressure, so the more versatile the translator, the better. In the fifties, British philosopher Arthur Toynbee claimed that the world is beginning to know more and more about less and less until soon we will know everything about nothing. Is translation approaching that point? If so, will it become like medicine where the patient (in our case the client) gets handed around from specialist to specialist before one of the remaining rare generalist breed discovers the hand hurt because of a thorn in the finger?

By excessive specialization, translators, especially those who translate to foreign languages, not only limit the amount of work they can receive—clients, including those in international business, are not sophisticated enough to distribute legal copy to one translator, financial to another, and technical specifications to a third. Because good versatile translators learn a little from every new task, their knowledge expands daily. Many who do not claim to specialize are often at least as good in a specialized area as are those who claim specialization after having worked in a subject area for a year or two. Because of their versatility, true generalists "know what they don't know" and learn it based on their vast general commercial, legal, technical and scientific education. This means that they are fully in compliance with the ATA Code of Ethical Business Practices which requires the translator to "... be a master of the target language ... have an excellent knowledge of the source language and the subject area to understand the message in depth...." They are the ones most useful to international trade because they understand a deal from beginning to end, including the engineering specifications but they can also work with the customer in adaptations, modifications, in cases of doubt talking to overseas agents, and more. They make good international business partners. Translation and international business have to become and be partners, in order to arrive at translations which serve their purpose.

6. Untranslatable images, cultures, legal word contents etc.

Every translator encounters images in the source which cannot be "just" translated but more often require "transthinking, transimaging." "What's *Fahrvergnügen?*" asked many Americans when the Volkswagen ads first appeared on TV. And we explained. In translations for immediate publication, there is no way to explain. Not every international firm has the millions it takes to splash a new word across TV screens until it becomes a buzzword. Because in translations for immediate dissemination, there is no room for explaining cultural, legal, and accounting systems and other differences in a footnote or long-winded translation, terminology must "hit the nail on the head." Translators must be highly resourceful in finding ever new solutions.

Translated headlines are normally produced in a manner very similar to that which copywriters use, and each "accepted" foreign language headline may be preceded by dozens that don't make it. In between, translators may repeatedly subject their "native" friends and relatives, both here and abroad, to boring advertising headlines, bouncing off on them numerous versions until a consensus is reached and the headline is not only understood but meets the intended purpose and "hits home." Then the client needs to be told what concept changes have been made, but generally international business relies on versatile talented translators to produce what it needs, whether through its advertising department or agency or directly. Even the best dictionaries won't help in these situations.

7. Dictionaries, whether on paper or on-line, are often not quite up-to-date, not sufficiently specialized, not specific enough for the level of audience, or not immediately available; alternatives may be expensive.

Many of the matters translated from a foreign language to English allow the translator to draw upon his knowledge enhanced by daily reading of one or more newspapers or journals, and, as mentioned, many are afforded the luxury of specializing. Libraries contain material in English on the same or similar subject, and above all, the client can actually help clarify terms through in-house personnel well familiar with the subject area being translated. All good translators to English have a "data bank" of colleagues and consultants who are not an ocean away. If the translator does not know that the *frappeur suppléant* is the equivalent of a "pinch hitter" in baseball, or what the ingredient is called that goes into beer, a green plant that is dried on some also unknown device, it will not take too many expensive phone calls to get the answers from someone who need not even know the source language.

Software terms in several European languages may pass through several stages, before a term "sticks." Computers may be verbally discussed in Germany using English terminology, but when the manuals are written, German terms prevail. This is aside from the fact that there may still be different terms for the same thing from different manufacturers and for different consumer levels. Only by buying or subscribing to journals in the foreign language is it possible to stay up-to-date, and even then, some may never show up, or the technical press may initially use wrong or English terms. The translator has to be inventive and not only use available reference works but once again closely cooperate with the manufacturer who may provide a consultant or contact person overseas to discuss and establish terminology.

Resources are inherently more expensive for a translator to a foreign language since phone calls and subscriptions cost more. There is still no guarantee that one's brother in Munich or Mexico City has a Post-It™-Note or a No. 2 pencil on his desk when called to establish beyond any doubt that the adhesive note has not (yet) acquired a German or Spanish name and that the pencil grading system is the same. Calls to several other overseas consultants may be required. This does not mean that the translator has accepted a job that is in a subject area with which he or she is not familiar. These things simply don't appear in ordinary dictionaries and not even erudite journals. It can, indeed, occur any day, even in the "easiest" translation, and it does, usually in a rush job at midnight for delivery to Europe at 8 o'clock in the morning.

When faced with translating fitness equipment to Dutch, two St. Louis translators recently learned that even their contacts in Holland were unable to tell them exactly what the equipment was called, although they knew well what they would do on the equipment. It took their Dutch friends' willingness to go to fitness clubs to determine what's called what and feed back the information in time to meet the translators' deadline. In spite of this, the manufacturer had a new twist to an old-established device, and the translators had to do a bit of intelligent adapting to make it sound new, innovative and attractive. Often the names under which equipment or instruments are sold are not the same ones that are contained in the patents, and occasionally the translator has to "invent" new terminology because the customer does not want to use the same nomenclature as the competition.

While the banding together in specialized interest or language groups, such as through the Divisions in ATA, may have provided some of the solutions to the discomfort felt by many translators to foreign languages over the years, one factor contributing to the desire for Divisions lies in the relative isolation with which many translator go about their trade. They maintain contact with colleagues, but many work for agencies which effectively prevent any contact between translator and customer. Inquiries and shop-talk on Flefo/Compuserve have perhaps alleviated some of the isolation problem, since there is now communication at least from translator to translator, and sometimes from outsiders here and abroad.

Whether in an actual translation situation or in a less structured setting, translators must learn not only to talk to fellow translators but to meet translation users in person, in public, to seek opportunities for educating them. We must go where business people meet and talk their language; we must show them that we are educated professionals who can participate in their conversations about business and world trade (and occasionally we may even have to feign interest in football, etc.). Whether we create these opportunities by getting involved in chambers of commerce, international trade associations, or other meetings of business executives does not really matter. When they learn to respect us as intelligent persons who understand their business they will also learn to respect us as professionals.

We must also start educating future users by talking to educators, school and university counselors, linguists, the media and others who continue to have misconceptions about our profession and about what translators do. Past attempts by translator associations at user education on a few sheets of paper or through films or videotapes about our work have at times been worthwhile efforts but have not been tremendously successful. We cannot wait for associations to do things for us. User education is the task of each and every translator.

At the same time, professional associations for translators and interpreters exist to promote the interests of their membership; this also means assisting translators in gaining pride in their knowledge and convincing them that they have a responsibility to help their association meet its goals in user education. Translators, especially those who deal with international trade, should make every possible effort to meet their clients at every opportunity, outside the actual job situation, in order to show the clients discreetly that they can talk shop with us, whether in a discussion on NAFTA or about export credits or the commercial situation in a specific country, that we are familiar with currencies and international banking, bills of lading and other export documentation, ISPO and European Community safety standards, that we do understand U.S. and international politics. We can also learn where our clients' best sources of information regarding specific problems may be (often as simple as the U.S. Department of Commerce or a local chamber of commerce or the trade attaché at a foreign embassy) and provide useful help through easily acquired knowledge.

Only when all of us make a concerted user education effort will we succeed in attaining the recognition the profession deserves. Don't expect miracles from your professional association, either your local one or your national ones—go out and do it yourself! Whether as a national association, as a special-interest division, as a local group, or as an individual, in our user education directed at international trade, we must realize that our first and foremost goal as translators should be to best serve our customers in every way possible.

By our user education, we can help our customers overcome the feeling that we are strange beings who happen to be able to "convert" a language, a job which most customers would prefer to avoid. Customers often feel ill at ease when they have to deal with translators because they are never quite certain about the product that they are buying. They would like to know what's under the frosting of the cake but are uneasy because they don't know how to sample it.

As in all good advertising, we must show our clients the value of our work under the aspects from which they derive the greatest benefit. Showing ourselves as knowledgeable partners is one of the ways we can make our customers feel more comfortable. Occasionally we will be given an opportunity to explain how we arrive at a good translation and to chat about the ingredients, when we are officially invited by a group to speak to them about translation. Speaking at schools is good, but speaking to an SBA arranged meeting, an international trade association or a chamber of commerce gathering provides a much more worthwhile audience to educate. Local translator/interpreter groups are excellent facilitators for arranging such "gigs." As long as we don't bore our audience to death with our specialized knowledge, we will be invited again.

Each individual translator should exude pride in the profession. We must not behave like underdogs but as professionals equal to other professionals needed by the U.S. business community in an international marketplace to an extent equal to that to which lawyers, CPAs, and export consultants are indispensable. We must show our customers that our highest goal is to help them further their goals, we must demonstrate that translation is not self-serving but that our purpose consists in helping them do business overseas in a better manner, we must show them what the bottom line of a good translation is. Needless to say that pays off in our own bottom line.

Section 3:

Ethics and the Profession

Professional Ethics for Court and Community Interpreters

NANCY SCHWEDA NICHOLSON

Although most professional organizations and associations have developed codes of ethics, the majority of these codes do not include concrete examples of particularly challenging and difficult situations which often confront both court and community interpreters. Rather, and necessarily, the guidelines are of a general nature in an attempt to set standards regarding important issues such as confidentiality and impartiality which apply to numerous circumstances. In addition to terminological, procedural, and subject matter problems (especially in legal and medical settings), interpreters face ethical dilemmas on a daily basis. These difficulties may be associated with the participants themselves (such as their respective roles and personalities) and/or they may be reflective of the nature of a specific situation (a courtroom setting or a mental health clinic). Here we examine several codes of ethics, select the canons mentioned most often, and illustrate these canons with examples of real-life ethical problems and their solutions.

I. Introduction

"Service providers cannot provide effective service for people with whom they cannot communicate. Non-English-speaking clients need, and have the right to, access to professional interpreters" (*Providing Services* n.d.:1). "Professional" is a key word in this quotation. All too often, interpretation services are furnished by self-styled "interpreters," those who speak two or more languages but lack training in techniques as well as duties and responsibilities.[1] As a result, serious mistakes and/or unconscionable breaches of ethics may occur without ever being noticed. Inasmuch as the great majority of attorneys and other service providers do not speak one of the languages involved, it is easy to understand how nearly impossible it is to check on the accuracy, completeness, and ethical behavior of the "interpreter." At least when trained professionals are employed, one can be fairly certain that accepted standards and procedures will be known to and followed by the interpreter.

Before continuing, it is useful to provide definitions of "court" and "community" interpreting. The Twin Cities Interpreter Project (TCIP), primarily involved with interpreter training for refugee mental health situations, defines "court" interpreting as: "courtroom communications among the defendant, lawyers, witnesses, and judge" ("Basic terminology" 1988:2). It is also important to add that court interpreting may also include interpretation outside of the formal courtroom setting, such as in an attorney's office or at a prison, generally in preparation for a case. "Community" interpreting is defined as: "everyday and emergency situations which refugees, other immigrants, and migrant laborers may encounter in their communication with bureaucrats, officials, police, employment counselors, school, public assistance and health care personnel of all kinds" ("Basic terminology" 1988:2). Most people distinguish between the two types of interpretation, but it could easily be argued that "community" interpreting does, in fact, encompass court interpreting as well (see Longley 1984). Therefore, "community" interpreting could be used as an all-inclusive term.[2] It is the author's opinion that court and community interpretation are often differentiated because court interpretation has enjoyed much attention and has greatly expanded (especially in the United States) since the passage of the *Court Interpreters Act* (Public Law 95-539) in 1978 (see Schweda Nicholson 1992; 1991; 1989; 1986). Now more than ever, judges and attorneys (especially in the United States District Courts, the trial court level of the federal judicial system) are generally aware of the law, its provisions, and the importance of ensuring due process for non-English-speaking defendants.

All over the United States, training programs for interpreters have been developed and implemented; moreover, the public has become more sensitized to and knowledgeable about the field due to a proliferation of newspaper articles and studies which examine ongoing problems and potential solutions. However, despite progress in the areas of general medical, mental health, and social services interpreting, for example, these types have not yet reached the stage of court interpreting with respect to education of service providers, interpreter training opportunities and standardization of services.

It is also worthy of mention that both court and community interpreting are differentiated from conference interpreting, a truly prestigious occupation, which has a relatively long and illustrious history (if one counts the pre-simultaneous days as well). Professional associations of conference interpreters such as the International Association of Conference Interpreters (AIIC), The American Association of Language Specialists (TAALS) and the American Society of Interpreters (ASI) are well-organized and established, having instituted clear and strict membership guidelines early on. As a result, conference interpreting does not share many of the problems connected with interpreting in everyday situations, as described above.

II. Codes of Ethics

Before proceeding to a discussion of the topics treated by various codes of ethics, it is useful to examine some pertinent data which were gathered by the New Jersey Supreme Court Task Force on Interpreter and Translation Services. The Task Force conducted a survey of New Jersey judges with respect to ethics among interpreters (*The Practices of Interpretation* 1983). It is interesting to note that only 25% of the judges responding expressed that they are "completely" satisfied with the interpreters' knowledge of ethical considerations. One judge wrote: "I didn't know they [interpreters] were governed by professional ethics" (1983:68). Examining the breakdown in the other categories with respect to "judges' satisfaction with interpreters' ethics," one notes that 42% are "over half" satisfied; 20% are "less than half" satisfied, and 13% are "not at all" satisfied (1983:69). The study concludes that "... while a minority (25%) of judges are completely satisfied with interpreters' ethical knowledge and performance, substantial dissatisfaction about interpreters' ethics prevails among the judges" (1983:69). These data, of course, are now ten years old. It would be interesting to conduct the survey once again to see if the judges' attitudes have changed, especially with the increased availability of training and testing opportunities in New Jersey.

A number of codes of ethics were consulted in the preparation of this paper: (1) the *Code of Professional Responsibility for Federal Court Interpret-*

ers (1993); (2) the *Translators' Code of Professional Conduct and Business Practices* (1992) and (3) the *Code of Ethical Practices and Professional Rights* (1967), both of the American Translators Association; (4) the *Code of Professional Conduct* and (5) *Personal Guidelines for Interpreters*, both of the Institute of Translation and Interpreting (London) (1988); (6) the *Code of Professional Responsibility for Interpreters, Transliterators and Translators* of the Administrative Office of the Courts, State of New Jersey (1990); (7) the *Proposed Code of Ethics for Interpreters in Mental Health for Refugees and Others* (Benhamida 1988); (8) the *Code of Ethics* of the California Court Interpreters Association (Undated); (9) the *Professional Code for Court Interpreters–Ethics and Practice* of the Court Interpreters and Translators Association (1982); (10) the *Code of Ethics* of the Registry of Interpreters for the Deaf (1979) and (11) the *Interim Regulations Implementing the Court Interpreters Amendments Act of 1988* (1988).

Seven of the most common areas covered by these codes are: (1) the interpreter's overall role; (2) competence and required skills; (3) impartiality; (4) completeness and accuracy; (5) conflicts of interest and grounds for disqualification; (6) confidentiality; and (7) continuing professional development. For purposes of discussion, each topic is treated individually, although some areas necessarily overlap with others. Related problems as well as their solutions are introduced as illustrations.

A. THE INTERPRETER'S OVERALL ROLE

Much discussion recently has centered on the role of the interpreter in various settings.[3] In essence, the interpreter bridges the gap between parties who would otherwise be unable to communicate. Don Barnes, retired Chief of Language Services at the U.S. Department of State, characterizes the role of the interpreter as similar to a "pane of glass," through which light passes without alteration or distortion (Personal communication, 1990). Continuing with the "pane of glass" analogy, one can say that the interpreter allows for the communication of ideas, once again, without modification, adjustment or misrepresentation. The TCIP's *Proposed Code* clearly states that "the interpreter's only function is to facilitate communication" (Benhamida 1988:5). In the same vein, Niska (1990) writes about the role of the interpreter, stressing that "the principle for information transfer is ... to conceal, to add or to change nothing" (12).

Ashworth (1990) discusses a technique used at the Japan American Institute of Management Science in Honolulu which goes beyond the "pane of glass" comparison. The method is based on a "synergistic model of management," stressing (1) the development of listening skills; (2) attention to each speaker's position on the issue; (3) synthesis of the views of all involved; and (4) consensus building (16). He refers to the interpreter as a "facilitator," one who allows both sides to talk **with** each other (as opposed to **at** each other). In order to increase the likelihood of mutual understanding, the facilitator employs (1) "reflection," during which he/she "reinterprets statements made by the American staff using a variety of English that is more likely comprehended by the Japanese staff" and (2) "clarification," which is "similar to reflection" and involves elucidation (16). Although "reflection" goes beyond the boundaries of the traditional interpreter's role, the facilitator does share many key characteristics with the interpreter, such as an awareness of the cultural differences between the Japanese and Americans, recognition of the meaning of non-verbal behavior in both societies, and the suppression of their personal opinions so they do not intrude during the facilitation process. However, it must be noted that this is a specialized training technique employed in a unique setting and, as such, cannot be compared to, for example, an adversarial courtroom situation, wherein the goal of the attorneys may be to confuse and mislead.

Astiz (1986) refers to an "adaptation role," one in which some interpreters believe that it is incumbent upon them to clarify and otherwise modify what is said because in their eyes, the individuals involved (such as witnesses or defendants) may not be able to grasp the meaning of the original language as it is formulated. In this connection, another side of the adaptation role is the alteration of what a witness says in order to make it more acceptable to the court, i.e., eliminating uncouth or vulgar expressions. Astiz further writes that some administrators and judges confirmed that interpreters often approved of the adaptation role and that they (the judges and administrators) were generally supportive of it as well. He concludes that

> ... with the appropriate professional training, interpreters would have known that the 'adaptation role' contradicts the expectation of accuracy, precision, and neutrality which are [sic] essential to the performance of their true task. (34)

Finally, Schneider (1992) refers to an "interpreter/conciliator," an individual who plays a critical role in conflict resolution, especially when intercultural and interracial hostilities arise among primarily immigrant groups who have limited English proficiency. Schneider is clear to distinguish between the traditional interpreter role and that of the "interpreter/conciliator." She does not suggest that all interpreters be conciliators as well; in fact, she states: "... it is conceivable that an interpreter, a conciliator, and an interpreter/conciliator may be used effectively together in a given situation" (63).

While the facilitator role, the adaptation role, and the interpreter/conciliator role may be appropriate in certain situations, it is important to stress that the "pane of glass" analogy is the one which most accurately reflects the most basic and fundamental function of the interpreter.

B. Competence and Required Skills

"Interpreters shall accept assignments using discretion with regard to skill, setting, and the consumers involved" (Benhamida 1988:6).

"We are bound, by the Code of professional conduct, to maintain at all times the highest standards.... That means ensuring, inter alia, that we have the **required** linguistic competence, the **required** interpreting skills, and the **required** experience and subject-knowledge for the job assigned" (emphasis in original) (*Personal Guidelines* 1990:1).

"Interpreters and translators shall accurately and completely represent their certifications, training and pertinent experience" (*Code of Professional Responsibility for Interpreters* 1990:4).

It is unfortunate but true that untrained interpreters probably never stop to ask themselves if, in fact, they are qualified to undertake a particular assignment. Inasmuch as the prevailing attitude among many foreign language speakers themselves, and service providers as well, is "anyone who speaks two languages can interpret," one often finds individuals who simply cannot fulfill their obligations to interpret completely and accurately. This failing may be due to a number of things: (1) the "interpreter's" level of linguistic competence in either or both the source and target languages is insufficient; (2) the "interpreter" is unskilled in the techniques of simultaneous and/or consecutive interpretation, including note-taking; (3) the "interpreter" is not knowledgeable about courtroom/medical procedures; and (4) the "interpreter" is not versed in the jargon and specialized terminology which are a large part of any legal or medical encounter. Astiz (1986:33) likens the use of an unqualified interpreter to having no interpretation at all: "We subscribe to the view that there is no legal difference in terms of meeting the constitutional guarantees of non-English-speaking individuals between refusal to provide interpreting services and use of incompetent interpreters. In both cases defendants are denied due process of law and the opportunity to cross-examine witnesses and victims."

C. IMPARTIALITY

> "Official court interpreters fulfill a special duty to interpret accurately and faithfully without indicating any personal bias, avoiding even the appearance of partiality" (*Code of Professional Responsibility for Federal* 1993:28).
>
> "[Interpreters] should be unobtrusive and unbiased, never revealing through word or gesture their own impression or opinion of the proceedings" (*Code of Professional Responsibility for Federal* 1993:29)
>
> "The interpreter should maintain an impartial attitude with defendants, witnesses, attorneys and families. He should neither conceive of himself nor permit himself to be used as an investigator for any party to a case. The interpreter should not 'take sides' or consider himself aligned with the prosecution or the defense" (*Professional Code* 1982:1).
>
> "Interpreters shall not interject or reveal their own feelings, moods, attitudes or beliefs while performing their professional duties" (*Code of Professional Responsibility for Interpreters* 1990:3).

Impartiality is yet another integral component of a code of ethics (Ashworth 1990; Longley 1984; Niska 1990; Schuker 1990). Interpreters, as human beings, cannot help but be moved by emotional testimony, disgusted when graphic crimes are described, or angered when they believe a witness to be lying. Moreover, when an interpreter works consistently with a particular client in doctor-patient interviews or interprets for a lengthy trial, it would be impossible not to form a personal opinion of the principals and their activities. However, although the interpreter may experience all of the aforementioned feelings, it is incumbent upon her **not** to allow her attitudes and reactions to become known to the parties involved.[4] She must never (via words, facial expressions, gestures, or tone of voice) expose her emotions in any way, shape or form. If, in fact, an interpreter finds that her personal feelings are interfering with her production of an accurate and complete interpretation, she should withdraw from the assignment.

Niska (1990) offers a telling example of how an interpreter permitted her personal opinions and beliefs to influence her rendition, which did not accurately represent the tone and demeanor of the government official involved. The interpreter was working at a hearing of a social welfare board in Sweden. The issue was a Finnish immigrant mother's desire to enroll her child in a Finnish-speaking pre-school instead of a Swedish-speaking one. At that time, Niska reports, the matter of mother-tongue education for immigrant groups was a controversial and emotional topic about which many people held strong opinions. The interpreter, who believed that a government official present was wrong to insist that the child's acculturation would be facilitated by attending a Swedish-speaking school, permitted her personal feelings to enter into her interpretation:

> "My view was very clear. The politician was talking through her hat about things she didn't understand. It was downright embarrassing to show such stupidity in public. What was I to do? I was torn between the urge to put the politician right, my reluctance to pass on her stupidity to the client, and the ethical requirement to interpret everything without saying what I thought myself.
>
> "My solution was that I **did** (emphasis in original) interpret everything, but both my intonation and choice of words conveyed very clearly that this was definitely not my own opinion, and that I realised the politician was not speaking through ill-will but through ignorance. Just how biased that interpreting was, I don't know" (14).

Moreover, a biased interpreter may (1) omit certain things altogether; (2) invent material which was never spoken; (3) alter what is said so as to help or harm one side or the other, and/or (4) emphasize matters which were not accentuated in the original version or, conversely, downplay a point which was clearly stressed.

D. COMPLETENESS AND ACCURACY

> "Interpreters and translators shall faithfully and accurately reproduce in the receptor language the closest natural equivalent of the source-language message without embellishment, omission or explanation" (*Code of Professional Responsibility for Interpreters* 1990:1).
>
> "[Interpreters] preserve the level of language used, and the ambiguities

and nuances of the speaker, without any editing" (*Code of Professional Responsibility for Federal* 1993:28).

"Interpret everything.... Accuracy is a must.... Interpreters should be able to stand by their interpretation, but if you find out that a mistake was made, take steps to correct it immediately" (*Code of Ethics* [undated]:2).

"Interpreters shall render the message faithfully, always conveying the content and spirit of the speaker, using language most readily understood by the person(s) whom they serve" (Benhamida 1988:3).

Discussion in Section II. C. of the shortcomings of a biased interpreter leads directly to the next topic: completeness and accuracy. The last quotation in the above list (Benhamida) merits further comment. The author believes that the final section, "using language most readily understood by the person(s) whom they serve" is misleading. Its wording may give the reader the impression that adjusting one's language (perhaps simplifying the vocabulary or breaking long sentences/questions down into more manageable, shorter items) is acceptable. Based on additional guidelines which are offered in the *Proposed Code* under this point, it is clear that Benhamida does not support the alteration of the message in any way:

"The level or style of language used in the source language shall be preserved in the target language. Simple, crude or obscene language shall not be dressed up nor shall sophisticated and erudite language be simplified" (4).

As an interpreter trainer, the author is often asked about choice of words, eliminating profanity, making ungrammatical items into grammatical ones, and otherwise altering material, all with the stated goal of making a witness or patient "look better" (more intelligent, worldly, educated or refined than he or she is). One trainee, who adamantly agreed with the above procedure, described his sentiments as representing a more "humanistic" approach to interpretation. The reader is once again referred to the "adaptation" role described in Section II. A. (Astiz 1986). Of course, one must surmise that interpreters who would consider altering material in the aforementioned ways and for the above reasons lack knowledge about the ethical constraints of their job. However, although training opportunities have expanded during the past fifteen years, it is still to be expected that many untrained interpreters step into American courtrooms every day and inaccurately represent the proceedings in one way or another.

Of course, there are times when the professional interpreter has every intention of rendering the source language material completely and accurately. However, due to the speaker's speed or poor enunciation on her part, the interpreter may simply miss some information. In instances such as these, the interpreter must ask the speaker to repeat, so as to ensure that the material will be rendered as spoken. In describing the lengthy Amoco Cadiz trial, Schuker states that "[t]he most common interpreter error was omission of some part of a long-winded statement. . . ." (1990:6). He offers an excellent example of a list of items which was probably uttered very quickly, thereby raising the possibility that the interpreter might miss one or more of its components. The list consisted of "boots, oilskins, shovels, rakes, plastic bags" (6). Schuker correctly states that, in another venue, (such as a conference situation) the interpreter might use a general term (in this case "cleanup equipment"), or could easily and acceptably say "boots, shovels, and so on" (6). However, inasmuch as this was a courtroom trial, each item had to be clearly enumerated with no omissions.

To offer a further example, the author was approached after a recent speech by a young lady who worked as a Punjabi interpreter (without the benefit of training, as her question will attest). She asked the author whether it would be permissible, during a trial, to substitute a more commonly known word for the one which the witness uttered. Her motivation for doing so was that "if I change this word, it will help to avoid about twenty more questions by the attorney" (Personal communication, November 7, 1992). Of course, the author responded that it is imperative that she interpret the word exactly as it was spoken. By changing even a seemingly inconsequential word, she risked distorting the image projected by the witness to the principals in the courtroom. Use of the particular word could indicate arcane knowledge on the witness's part or, conversely, could mark that he or she was poorly educated, unrefined, or any number of things. The point is that, by changing or altering what is said, one takes the chance of misrepresenting that person to those who are in the process of evaluating his or her credibility and general demeanor (see also Astiz 1986; "How to best" 1990; and *Interpreting and Translating as Professions* 1984).

With respect to medical interpretation, Ergueta 1992 asks, "Should it be the interpreter's responsibility to simplify medical language, or should the doctors and nurses make an effort to use everyday expressions?" (12). She correctly concludes that the interpreter is not the individual who should alter what is said but rather, it is incumbent on the health care professional to make statements and ask questions in a clear and comprehensible fashion unless he or she wishes to risk misunderstanding or perhaps even alienation or embarrassment on the part of the patient.

Especially in mental health interviews or when a medical patient is under extreme stress as a result of an injury or shock, individuals may say things that are nonsensical, speech may be disjointed, and jumping from one topic to another may hinder comprehension. Normal syntax and grammar may be disrupted, so much so that it is impossible for the interpreter to grasp the meaning of what is being said. In instances such as these, it is important for the interpreter to interpret exactly what is said. It is not the interpreter's job to try to make sense out of things that may sound "crazy"; it is her responsibility to interpret for the health care provider who will, in turn, evaluate the patient based upon his or her demeanor and the language used. Schuker 1990 writes, "The interpreter is thus not free to select syntactical and lexical forms solely according to his sense of the target language's genius; he is also constrained to respect the forms already used in the conversation" (11).

E. CONFLICTS OF INTEREST AND DISQUALIFICATION

> "Interpreters shall disclose to the court, and to the parties in a case, any prior involvement with that case, or private involvement with the parties or others significantly involved in the case" (*Code of Professional Responsibility for Federal* 1993:27).

> "No attorney, probation supervisor or investigator, police officer, therapist, social worker, or other professional should interpret in any proceeding or any court support service in which he or she is professionally involved with a party to the matter" *Code of Professional Responsibility for Interpreters* 1990:2).

> "Before being sworn to serve in a case, an interpreter shall be required to disclose to the court and to the parties any prior involvement with the case or with any party or witness involved therein" (*Interim Regulations* 1988:6).

> "[Interpreters] accurately state their qualifications and refuse any assignment for which they are not qualified or under conditions which substantially impair their effectiveness" and "Interpreters have the duty to call to the attention of the court any factors or

conditions which adversely affect their ability to perform adequately" (*Code of Professional Responsibility for Federal* 1993:28).

As evidenced by the passages quoted, there are two key areas regarding disqualification: (1) disqualification because of prior involvement with a party in a case; and (2) disqualification because of linguistic, terminological, and/or personal difficulties with respect to an assignment.

It goes without saying that a potential interpreter's contact with anyone related to a case should be known to the court. Often, a professional interpreter will disqualify herself based on these grounds after discussing the nature of the involvement with the judge and other principals.

An important and recurring problem area regarding conflict of interest is that of having a law enforcement officer act as an interpreter for a witness or suspect (Schweda Nicholson 1989). A very recent occurrence illustrates this point. After the World Trade Center bombing in New York City, many non-English-speaking suspects were arrested. When one of them, Mohammed Salameh, was to be arraigned in Federal court, no federally-certified interpreter was available.[5] As such, an FBI agent, the only Arabic-speaking individual who could be located at the time, was called on to act as the interpreter. Understandably, the defendant felt uncomfortable in this situation. He confided to his lawyer that he believed the "interpreter" was offering a summary of what was said rather than providing a true simultaneous interpretation. Moreover, the defendant was prevented from speaking in private with his attorney prior to the arraignment (unless he wished to use the FBI agent as an "interpreter") because the FBI agent was, of course, an employee of the prosecution (Sowchek 1993). This is not to say that the FBI agent was not performing as he should, but the potential for a conflict of interest in such a situation is great. Certainly, the defendant would immediately fear that anything he wished to say to his attorney through the "interpreter" would immediately be relayed to the prosecution. This is a shocking occurrence to the author, especially because it occurred in a Federal court.[6] It seems clear that the judge should never have allowed the FBI agent to act as the "interpreter." First of all, an impartial interpreter is required, certainly one who has no interest in the outcome of the case. Second, the due process rights of the defendant were denied because he was unable to communicate with counsel without risking a breach of his right to confidentiality. Third, the qualifications of the "interpreter" are in question. Perhaps the FBI agent is a fluent bilingual in Arabic/English (although we cannot be sure of even his language ability), but he probably knows very little or nothing about the techniques of simultaneous and consecutive interpretation, not to mention the numerous ethical considerations which necessarily play a role in such a setting. Having no knowledge of this situation other than that provided in this short article, it appears clear to the author that the judge should not have continued the case until a professional interpreter could be found. Moreover, one has to wonder why arrangements for a suitable interpreter were not made in advance. Certainly, the Clerk of the Court knew that this suspect was going to be arraigned.

It is also possible that an interpreter may feel herself becoming personally involved in a case or with a patient, threatening her impartiality and objectivity. Moreover, related to "competence and required skills," if an interpreter is in the middle of a court case or has begun to work with a doctor and patient in medical interviews and suddenly realizes that the material has become too difficult or that an unanticipated subject requiring arcane knowledge has arisen, she must disqualify herself. In a related but different situation, if the interpreter feels at all uncomfortable (to the extent that she cannot proceed in a professional manner) with the subject matter, perhaps because a witness uses profanity and discusses distasteful things, it is also a clear-cut reason for disqualification. Anything such as this which could interfere with a true and faithful rendition requires that she ask to be excused from the case.

A lengthy murder trial in Wilmington, Delaware, involving Chinese/English interpretation presented particular challenges for the interpreters. During testimony by a key witness (Mr. Chen), the interpreter was, at times, unable to interpret what was said, and literally turned to the court and stated "I can't translate that" (Caddell 1991:B1). It appears that the interpreter did not offer to disqualify himself. The article states that the judge, the two prosecutors, and the defense attorney met for a number of hours and reached the decision that the trial would continue with a different interpreter. The interpreter in question is not mentioned as being in attendance at this meeting. As a result, the interpreter was excused and, although it may appear obvious that the individual doing the interpreting was having comprehension and expression difficulties, the article does not explicitly state the reasons for changing interpreters. However, Caddell concludes by describing Chen's linguistic demeanor which offers a clue to the possible problems encountered: "[Chen] stutters, speaks a Shanghai version of the Mandarin dialect, and somehow acquired a slight Brooklyn accent from his time in New York City" (1991:B2).

F. CONFIDENTIALITY

> "Interpreters and translators shall protect the confidentiality of all privileged or other confidential information which they obtain during the course of their professional duties" (*Code of Professional Responsibility for Interpreters* 1988:4).

> "Interpreters shall keep all assignment-related information strictly confidential" (Benhamida 1988:3).

> "I will safeguard the interests of my clients as my own and divulge no confidential information" (*Translators' Code* 1992: no page number).

Confidentiality is a key component of all codes of ethics which pertain to interpreters and translators. For example, when an interpreter assists a non-English-speaking defendant or witness to communicate with counsel, she is bound to protect attorney-client privilege by refraining from discussing all that transpires during the interview. Inasmuch as interpreters are often members of the immigrant community which they serve, there may be pressure from other group members to speak about what happened during confidential meetings. The author learned that this is often the case among Southeast Asian refugee groups when she taught an intensive interpretation course at the University of Minnesota in 1991. Instructional sessions stressed that, in order to gain and maintain the trust and respect of their countrymen and women, it is imperative that the interpreters not fall prey to those who wish to learn information about matters which are none of their business. This also raises the issue of the inappropriateness of having a relative or friend interpret. This procedure, unfortunately, is still quite common due to (1) the lack of organized interpreter services in many legal and medical settings and also (2) the service provider's ignorance of the dangers involved in using such a person. Moreover, having a relative or friend act as an interpreter for a client relieves the service provider of the responsibility of locating and paying a professional interpreter. "It still very often happens that neighbours, family, friends, even underaged immigrant children, must help with interpreting when an immigrant visits a doctor. That this is accepted and even encouraged by some institutions ('you could bring someone to interpret for you') is ... a symptom of ignorance combined with a large measure of indifference towards the people involved" (Niska 1990:12). Certainly, this situation makes it easy for the service provider because no extra effort is required on her part; however, these individuals often do not realize that using such a person as an interpreter can have disastrous consequences. "Many patients have complained that their rights of confidentiality have been violated by the relative or friend who served as an interpreter" (Ergueta 1992:12). Not only is the quality of interpretation in question in such a situation, but the fact that the *ad hoc* interpreter has a personal interest in the case may color her interpretation and/or provide her with gossip material for post-interview discussions with other friends or family members. "Family members or friends of the patient should not be used as interpreters because they lack the appropriate training, and most importantly, because they lack the objectivity needed to perform the interpreting tasks without interfering in the assessment or treatment process" (Garcia-Peltoniemi and Egli 1988:1).

G. Continuing Professional Development

"Interpreters and translators should continually improve their skills and knowledge and shall keep informed of all statutes, rules of court and policies of the Judiciary which relate to the performance of their professional duties" (*Code of Professional Responsibility for Interpreters* 1990:4).

"An interpreter shall strive to continually maintain and upgrade the professional knowledge required to perform the task or assignment accurately" (*Code of Ethics* (undated):1).

"Interpreters shall strive to further knowledge and skills through participation in workshops, professional meetings, interactions with professional colleagues, and reading of current literature in the field of intercultural communication, especially interpreting and translating" (Benhamida 1988:8).

Ongoing learning and upgrading of skills are important requirements for interpreters ("How to best" 1990; Niska 1990). With the advent of enhanced training opportunities, interpreters have more options available to them for continual improvement. In this connection, they can take advantage of courses which teach about unfamiliar subject matter areas. For example, a court interpreter who wishes to become involved in medical and mental health interpreting can register for a course designed to meet those specialized needs. Of course, the basic consecutive and simultaneous skills can be applied to any interpretation situation; however, terminology and procedures differ from one setting to the next. Working with a psychiatrist in a mental health evaluation using consecutive interpretation is certainly very different from simultaneous courtroom work. An interview between doctor and patient may or may not be adversarial. A patient may be disoriented, alert, or may alternate between periods of lucidity and times when he or she is oblivious to the surroundings. All of these factors present special challenges to the medical/mental health interpreter and can be treated in a training course.

In addition to attending formal classes offered by universities and other institutions of higher education, interpreters may also continue their professional development by participating in workshops and seminars which are often sponsored by local chapters of professional organizations. The aforementioned courses and seminars are an excellent option for those who have access to them. On the other hand, it is also possible for interpreters to work alone or with a colleague to strengthen their abilities. For example, interpreters can independently increase their general knowledge and familiarity with specialized terminology by reading (in **all** of their working languages) and by following changes in laws which are pertinent to their work. Moreover, interpreting skills can be maintained by practicing simultaneous and consecutive during the news, special interview programs (like "Face the Nation" and "This Week with David Brinkley"), and perhaps, if available, by watching cable courtroom channels which broadcast trials as they take place. Considering the fact the video cassette recorders have become ubiquitous in American society, the interpreter can record a trial and then stop the tape and interpret for the judge, witnesses, and attorneys. This type of practice (which is as close to real life as possible) is invaluable for the serious interpreter interested in maintaining and improving language and interpretation competencies. Interpreters can also enrich their knowledge base by exchanging ideas and strategies with colleagues, and by keeping abreast of political, social, and cultural changes in countries where their languages are spoken. The latter can be accomplished either on one's own or in consultation with colleagues who, for example, may just be returning from a visit to a particular country. Moreover, in this connection, it can be very helpful for interpreters to speak with individuals who have just arrived in the United States from, for example, El Salvador and Nicaragua. This is especially true if the interpreter, perhaps a native Spanish-speaker, has lived in this country for a number of years ("Outlines of videotape topics" 1988:7).

Regarding the availability of courses, the University of Delaware has launched a series of summer seminars which are appropriate for beginners and experienced individuals alike. For example, students in the 1992 seminar included conference interpreters who wanted additional exposure to consecutive interpretation (especially note-taking) with the goal of becoming more involved in courtroom and medical work. On the other hand, the group also counted among its members those who had been working strictly in consecutive and who wanted to acquire basic simultaneous skills. It is clear that even seasoned interpreters benefit significantly from continuing education, as it is often possible to incorporate techniques successfully used by others into one's own repertoire.

III. Conclusion

The current paper has examined a number of interpreter codes of ethics, analyzing and highlighting specific sections which play a critical role in any interpretation setting. Not by any means exhaustive in its treatment of topics, the article has offered a discussion of some of the most common problems and suggested solutions in the area of interpreter ethics.

Ethical issues arise in every type of community interpreting situation, from the most simple, straightforward medical history interview to the most complex, involved courtroom trial. As such, it is incumbent upon the interpreter to strictly adhere to the codes of ethics which have been developed, many of them relatively recently. Most people think only of language issues and interpreting skills when considering the task of the interpreter; however, it is clear that the maintenance of high ethical standards plays a definitive role in the interpretation profession.

NOTES

[1] Benhamida et al. (1988) refer to this type of *ad hoc* interpreting as "natural interpreting" ("Basic terminology":1).

[2] With respect to terminology referring to different types of interpretation and interpreters, Niska (1990) writes about "contact" interpreting in Sweden. He states that it is "... a new type of interpreting with special circumstances that differ from those of international conference or business interpreting" (2). Niska describes "contact" interpreting as one which occurs "... during non-Swedish-speakers' contact with authorities, institutions, and organisations"(2). He stresses that more has been done in Sweden to provide interpreter services for immigrants than anywhere else in the world.

[3] In addition to the various interpreter roles examined in this section, please see Gehrke 1989 for a discussion of interpreting for children.

[4] The author uses the pronouns "her" and "she" to refer to interpreters in the singular inasmuch as the great majority of interpreters today are women.

[5] No Federal Certification Examination currently exists for the Arabic/English language combination. There are, however, Federal Certification Examinations for Spanish/English, Navaho/English, and Haitian Creole/English.

[6] Since passage of the *Court Interpreters Act* in 1978, the Federal courts have become far more sensitive to language issues. For example, most courtroom personnel know that it is important to utilize a professional interpreter, one who is aware of not only the techniques of interpretation but also of the duties and responsibilities of the profession, especially with respect to confidentiality, impartiality, completeness and accuracy. It surprises the author that a Federal judge would have permitted an individual with such obvious ties to the prosecution (and, as such, a vested interest in the outcome of the case) to act as the interpreter.

REFERENCES

Ashworth, David. "A risk-taking role for the interpreter." *ATA Chronicle* October (1990): 16-17.
Astiz, Carlos. "But they don't speak the language." *The Judge's Journal* Spring (1986): 32-35, 56.
Barnes, Donald, Personal communication, January 14, 1990. "Basic terminology for the interpreting profession." In Benhamida et al. 1988, 3 pages.
Benhamida, Laurel, Bruce Downing, Eric Egli, and Zhu Yao. *Refugee Mental Health: Interpreting in Refugee Mental Health Settings: Video Workbook*. Minneapolis: Univ. of Minnesota Refugee Assistance Program–Mental Health Technical Assistance Center, 1988.
Benhamida, Laurel. "Proposed Code of Ethics for Interpreters in Mental Health for Refugees and Others." *Refugee Mental Health: Interpreting in Refugee Mental Health Settings: Video Workbook*, 8 pages. Minneapolis: Univ. of Minnesota Refugee Assistance Program–Mental Health Technical Assistance Center, 1988.
Code of Ethical Practices and Professional Rights. Arlington, VA: American Translators Association, 1967.
Code of Ethics. Healdsburg, CA: California Court Interpreters Association. Undated.
Code of Ethics. Silver Spring, MD: Registry of Interpreters for the Deaf, 1979.
Code of Professional Conduct. London: Institute of Translation and Interpreting, 1988.
Code of Professional Responsibility for Federal Court Interpreters. Washington, D.C.: Administrative Office of the United States Courts, 1993.
Code of Professional Responsibility for Interpreters, Transliterators, and Translators. Trenton, NJ: Administrative Office of the Courts, State of New Jersey, 1990.
Court Interpreters Act of 1978. (Public Law 95-539). Title 28, Sections 1827 and 1828, .539.
Ergueta, Elizabeth. "Hospital interpreting." *The Jerome Quarterly* 7.2 (1992): 12-13.
Garcia-Peltoniemi, Rosa and Eric Egli. "Guidelines for working with interpreters." *Refugee Mental Health: Interpreting in Refugee Mental Health Settings: Video Workbook*, 4 pages. Minneapolis: Univ. of Minnesota Refugee Assistance Program–Mental Health Technical Assistance Center, 1988.
Gehrke, Monica. "Preparing undergraduates for community interpreting." *The Jerome Quarterly* 4.3 (1989): 7-8, 15.
"How to best use an interpreter to your advantage." *Court Interpreters Gazette*, Vol. 4, June 1 (1990): 1-2.

Interim Regulations Implementing the Court Interpreters Amendments Act of 1988. Washington, D.C: Administrative Office of the United States Courts, 1988.
Interpreting and Translating as Professions. (Background Report #21). Trenton, NJ: Supreme Court Task Force on Interpreter and Translation Services, 1984.
Longley, Patricia. "What is a community interpreter?" *The Incorporated Linguist* 23.3 (1984): 178-81.
Niska, Helge. "A new breed of interpreter for immigrants." Trans. Tim Crosfield. Stockholm, Sweden: Institute for Interpretation and Translation Studies, Stockholm Univ., 1990.
"Outlines of videotape topics." In Benhamida et al., 7 pages, 1988.
Personal Guidelines for Interpreters. London: Institute for Translation and Interpreting, 1990.
Professional Code for Court Interpreters—Ethics and Practice. New York: Court Interpreters and Translators Association, 1982.
Providing Services With an Interpreter. Honolulu, HI: Bilingual Access Line, undated.
Schneider, P. Diane. "Interpreter/conciliator, an evolving function." *Proceedings of the 1992 American Translators Association Conference.* Ed. Edith F. Losa. Medford, NJ: Learned Information, Inc., 1992. 57-64.
Schuker, Théodore. "Interpreting in the Amoco Cadiz case." *The Jerome Quarterly* 6.1 (1990): 3-11, 15.
Schweda Nicholson, Nancy. "Interpretation services for lesser-used languages in the United States Courts: A language planning perspective." *Language Problems and Language Planning* 16.1 (1992): 38-52.
———. "Policy-making for Spanish court interpretation services." *Socio-linguistics of the Spanish-Speaking World.* Tempe, AZ: Bilingual Press, 1991: 329-48.
———. "Ad hoc interpreters in the United States: Equality, inequality, quality?" *Meta* 34.4 (1989): 711-23.
———. "Language planning and policy development for court interpretation services in the United States." *Language Problems and Language Planning* 10.2 (1986): 140-57.
Sowchek, Ellen. "News of the profession." *Gotham Translator* May (1993). Rpt. in ATA Chronicle June (1993): 5.
The Practices of Interpretation and Translation in New Jersey's Courts, The Judges' Point of View: A Survey of Trial Judges. (Background Report #9). Trenton, NJ: Supreme Court Task Force on Interpreter and Translation Services, 1983.
Translators' Code of Professional Conduct and Business Practices. Arlington, VA: American Translators Association, 1992.

Ethics for Translators and Translation Businesses

GABE BOKOR

What is "Translator Ethics?"

Much has been said lately about ethics in government and business, medical ethics and even ethics in international relations. In most cases these discussions are centered not on the philosophical or religious aspects of ethics, but on rational rules that make human intercourse possible without certain groups or individuals taking undue advantage of other groups or individuals. In particular, business ethics have come to denote fairness in the relationship between vendors and buyers of goods and services, among individuals and businesses in the same industry (colleagues and competitors), as well as between businesses and society at large. These relationships are governed by each country's laws, by certain international laws and accepted principles, as well as by the standards established by different professional and business organizations.

Although the standards for the translation industry do not basically differ from those of any other, ours have a few peculiarities that warrant the existence of the term "translator ethics" and of a "Translators' Code of Professional Conduct and Business Practices" (Ethics Code—see box).

One of these peculiarities is the elusive nature of the product we sell, which is not the sheets of paper (or computer diskettes) we actually deliver to our customers, but the skill acquired through years of language and subject matter studies and practice, as well as the time and effort expended to produce an expert translation. Selling these skills and their result (the translation) to customers who often cannot correctly evaluate them requires a unique degree of trust in the translator-client relationship and a mechanism to prevent and, if necessary, resolve conflicts.

Contrary to the situation in many foreign countries, the profession of translator in the U.S. is an unregulated one. No official certification exists, and credentials such as college degrees in translation or ATA accreditation are neither necessary for practicing the profession nor sufficient to assure the client that the translator has adequate qualifications to perform the job at hand.

While the client often has to trust the translator's representation concerning his or her qualifications and the quality of the work delivered, the translator is just as often expected to deliver hundreds and even thousands of dollars' worth of "merchandise" on credit and which cannot be repossessed, based on a simple phone call from a stranger located half a continent away.

Translation providers are typically individuals with little or no business or legal training or small businesses with limited resources, which have often grown from their owners' freelance practice. Translation users, on the other hand, often buy translations as they do paper clips or other commodities, and, since translations are usually only a small fraction of their total purchases, they seldom have adequate procedures for dealing with special translation-related issues.

The possibilities of a translator and client misunderstanding each other's expectations and of the relationship ending in conflict are endless. What is surprising is the relative rarity of serious disputes despite conditions that virtually call for them.

Meeting Each Other's Expectations

The concept of ethics and proper business practices means different things to the different parties of a business relationship involving translators and translations.

To the translation buyer it means that the translator is qualified to perform the work he or she undertakes, that the work is performed conscientiously, possible problems arising during the performance of the work are openly discussed with the customer, and the finished translation is delivered on time in the form requested. If the translation is supplied by a middleman (bureau), the latter is expected to select the proper translator for the job, check the quality of the translation and furnish a finished product that conforms to the final customer's specifications.

To the translator it means that the customer's expectations are clearly spelled out from the outset and not changed in mid-course without adequate compensation; that aid is given if requested and possible during the work and feedback given after delivery of the work. The translator expects to be paid as agreed upon, in a timely manner (usually within 30 days from the invoice date).

To the middleman (who is both a buyer and a seller of the translation) it means, in addition to the above-mentioned points, that the translator respects and does not interfere with the middleman's relationship with the final customer.

To all parties it means that all relevant parameters of the job are clearly spelled out before work is begun and strictly observed. More importantly, it means that all parties benefit from the transaction and none is, or feels, exploited by the other(s).

The ideal translator/translation buyer relationship is a long-term one, where the parties learn about each other's special requirements and expectations as they work together and thus reinforce the relationship.

An Ounce of Prevention

Although serious disputes between translators and translation buyers are relatively infrequent, most of those that do occur are due to the parties' failure to understand the expectations of the other party to the transaction. Details often not clarified when a job is assigned to a translator include:

1. What is to be translated (keyboarded):

   Numerical tables?
   Untranslatables (names, addresses, trademarks, etc.)?
   Target-language text in source-language document?
   Bibliography (transliteration of foreign-language titles?)
   American/metric conversions?
   Repeated portions, abstracts, bibliography, etc.?

2. Formatting

   What level of formatting is required? With today's word-processing software, formatting may range from unformatted text-only to quasi-typesetting.
   Tables?

Figures (pasteup? If captions to figures or tables are keyed, who does the keying and how is it paid for?)

3. Quantification

   Word, character, line or page count?
   Source or target language?
   What word-counting utility? (How is a "word" defined? Some utilities do not count numbers, others do not count one- or two-letter words)
   How is non-translation keyboarding (numbers, proper names, target-language text in the source-language document) quantified and paid for?

4. Research, consultation

   If the text is not clear and clarification from the client is required, who pays for the extra cost involved?

5. Presentation/delivery

   Hard copy, modem, disk, fax, overnight courier?
   Deadline: Date of mailing or job at client's premises?
   Payment: X days from delivery or invoice date *(regardless* of whether or when the translator's client is paid by a third party).

Most of these questions are raised in the *Standard Contract* proposed by Jane E. Maier and discussed in her article elsewhere in this volume. The more each of these issues is discussed and clarified *before* translation work is started, the better the chances are for a smooth, mutually satisfying relationship between translator and translation buyer.

While most of the problems in the translator-client relationship are not really ethical in nature, but rather a question of sound business practice, translators do face ethical problems, to which codes such as ATA's "Translators' Code of Professional Conduct and Business Practices" seldom provide an answer. Such problems include the dilemma of whether a text that clashes with the beliefs of the translator should be accepted for translation. I personally do not think that a professional organization can or should establish standards regulating behavior that largely depends on subjective elements. While illegal action should not be abetted or condoned by translators, those cases not defined by law must be decided by each person's own individual conscience.

Ethics and ATA

ATA has placed great emphasis on ethics since its very inception. In fact, shortly after its establishment, one of the founding members, Henry Fischbach, set about drafting a code of ethics for the Association. The code was based on the Code of the American Medical Writers Association, of which both Alexander Gode and Henry were members and from which they both borrowed some ideas when they founded ATA. Furthermore, a manifestation of the importance given to ethical conduct is the provision in ATA's Bylaws that past presidents of the organization are automatically entitled to serve on its Ethics Committee. Historically, most Ethics Committee Chairs have been selected from among past presidents.

Since ATA's membership includes people with different backgrounds, the perception of the role of the Ethics Committee has been different even from one Ethics Chair to another. An informal survey of five past Ethics Chairs also revealed considerable differences between (a) what they perceived as the main function of their Committee, (b) what they thought most ATA members expected from the Committee and (c) what they actually spent most time and effort on during their tenure. See Table 1 for the summarized results of this survey (respondents arranged in no particular order).

As can be seen from the table, while most former Ethics Committee Chairs cannot agree about what they regard as the main function of the Ethics Committee, "protecting translators against abuse (including non-payment) by bureaus and other translation users" ranks high with all of them in terms of time and effort spent, as well as in perceived importance by ATA membership.

My own view of the function of the Ethics Committee within the ATA is reflected in the current version of the "Translators' Code of Professional Conduct and Business Practices," which was approved during my term as Chair. (It appears at the end of this article.) I have defended a pragmatic approach to ethics and the importance of correct business practices that serve the best interests of both translators and translation users. We must shed the perception that translators are subordinate to translation buyers and replace it with sound practices based on mutual respect and a community of interests. We must be professionals not only as translators, but also as business people, whether freelances or bureaus, bound by the same rights and obligations that apply to the parties of any other business transaction.

TABLE 1

	Chair #1	Chair #2	Chair #3	Chair #4	Chair #5
1. What is, in your view, the main purpose of ATA's Ethics Committee?					
2. As Ethics Chair, what took most of your time and effort?					
3. In your opinion, what does the majority of ATA members expect from the Ethics Committee? Items ranked from [1]–most important to [6]–least important					
a) Monitoring observance of ethical behavior by translators	6,6,6	5,4,4	6,2,-	2,4,5	1,2,2
b) Educating translators about ethics	4,5.4	4,5,5	3,2,-	1,5,3	2,-,-
c) Educating translators about correct business practices	5,4,5	1,3,2	1,2,-	4,2,2	6,-,-
d) Enforcing ATA's Bylaws and policies	1,3,1	3,2,3	5,6,-	5,3,4	4,3,3
e) Protecting translators against abuses (including non-payment) by bureaus and other translation users	3,2,3	2,1,1	4,1,1	2,1,1	3,1,1
f) Other (specify)	2[1],1[1],2[1]	-	2[2]	-	5[3],4[4]

[1] Arbitrating disputes among translators and translation users.
[2] Educating translators and translation users about the proper translator-user relationship
[3] Monitoring translators' (including bureaus') advertising
[4] Monitoring bureaus' advertisements

As the translation industry becomes more and more international, translators will have to learn not only the business rules and customs of their own country, but also those of their clients, wherever they may be located. International business involving intangible goods has few universally accepted rules, and modern technology (modems, facsimile machines) has introduced new elements that further complicate these rules. This makes it even more important for translators to adhere to common-sense practices rather than abstract ideologies in order to be successful.

The American Translators Association

Translators' Code of Professional Conduct and Business Practices

I. As a translator, I stand between two languages and act as a bridge for the free passage of ideas from one side to the other. Because my knowledge, skill, and discretion are essential to intellectual commerce, I commit myself to the highest standards of performance, ethical behavior, and sound business practice.

1. I will endeavor to translate with utmost accuracy and fidelity, so that I convey to the readers of the translation the same meaning and spirit the original conveyed to me. I acknowledge that this level of excellence requires:
    a) mastery of the target language equivalent to that of an educated native speaker;
    b) up-to-date knowledge of the source language and the subject area sufficient to understand the message;
    c) continued efforts to improve my professional skills and to broaden and deepen my knowledge.
2. I will be truthful about my qualifications and business practices and will not accept any assignment for which I am not fully qualified, without the express consent of my client.
3. I will safeguard the interests of my clients as my own and divulge no confidential information.
4. I derive no personal profit or financial gain from confidential information I receive in my professional capacity.
5. I will clarify all aspects of my contractual relationship with my client, preferably in writing, prior to performing any assignment and will strictly adhere to the agreed terms.
6. I will notify my clients of any unresolved difficulties I may encounter in the performance of the assignment.
7. I will use a client's name as a reference only if I am prepared to direct the prospective client to the individual who can attest to the quality of my work.
8. I will respect and refrain from interfering with the business relationship that exists between my client and my client's client.

II. As an employer of translators or as one who contracts assignments to translators, I will uphold the above standards in conducting my business. I further commit myself to the following fair practices in dealing with translators:

1. I will clarify all aspects of my contractual relationship with the translator and state my expectations regarding the assignment from the outset, preferably in writing.
2. I will strictly adhere to the agreed terms of this relationship, including the payment deadline, and will not capriciously change the job specifications after the translator's work has begun.
3. I will not require translators to do unpaid work against the prospect of a paid assignment.
4. I will deal directly with the translator in the event of any dispute about an assignment; if we fail to resolve the problem, we will seek an arbitrator.
5. I will not use the translator's credentials in bidding for a job or promoting my business without the translator's consent or without the bona fide intention to use the translator's services.
6. In the case of translations intended for publication or performance, I will grant translators recognition of the kind traditionally granted authors, including mention of their name on the title page and jacket of the published translation or in the theater program and in the advertising of the work.
7. In the case of commercially published or produced works, I acknowledge the translators' right to approve or reject any substantial changes in the translated text, or, alternatively, to have their name removed from the work without prejudice to the agreed payment.

Section 4:

Challenges of Technology

The Issues
of Machine Translation

MURIEL VASCONCELLOS

Machine translation! The very words evoke a range of emotions from disdain, fear, and disbelief to bedazzlement and thrilled expectation. They also raise deep doubts, aesthetic and even moral. And they bring up myriad practical questions about what "MT" really *is.*

Broadly speaking, MT is *the technology whereby computers attempt to model the human process of translating between natural languages.* Although human beings almost always intervene at different points in the job stream, especially at the end, the underlying process is automatic: the machine is in charge of the transition from one language to the other.

Whether or not MT really does produce translation, and what its impact may or may not be for "human" translators will be discussed in the pages that follow. The profession can expect to be faced with an increasingly broad spectrum of issues begotten by this technology. These issues will get larger and take on new colors and flavors as the use of MT takes a quantum leap forward with the advent of affordable software on desktop PCs, available for all and sundry to experiment with.

Many humanists, including translators, find abhorrent the very idea of turning over to a computer a process as profoundly creative as translation. Indeed, a sensitive translation takes into account every thread of implication in a text, weighs its relative importance within the entire fabric of communicative systems in the source language, and reproduces the same nuances in the target language—necessarily a different set of systems—with all proportions kept. So daunting is the challenge that an eminent philosopher once referred to translation as "probably the most complex type of event yet produced in the evolution of the cosmos" (Richards 1953).

At bottom, the objection to MT is that the computer is presumed to *generate* the translation. And in fact the defining characteristic of MT has always been that the computer generates the output—i.e., so-called "translations" of natural language text fed to it at the input end—even though the process almost always involves some form of human assistance as well. On the other hand, there has been little or no objection to MT's counterpoint, *machine-aided translation,* in which the human being generates the translation and enlists the computer to speed up the task. In the first case the computer has an active role, whereas in the latter it is passive, standing by like a well-trained butler waiting to do its master's bidding. These, at least, are the two ends of the spectrum; recent technology is beginning to make the distinction less clear-cut. Today once-passive data bases are serving up increasingly larger chunks of text—for example, matches of translations in progress drawn from text stored in memory—while on the other hand sophisticated MT systems are planning to tap into terminological knowledge bases so that they can make smarter choices as they crunch their sentences (Schütz and Ripplinger 1993; Mitamura, Nyberg, and Carbonell 1993).

For many admirers of the translation process, a translation generated by computer is, a priori, a bumptious affront to human creativity. Others who do not feel quite so strongly accept that MT might be used in some circumstances but worry about its dehumanizing effect on translators, believing that it will turn them into slaves to the machine. Or worse still, they fear that the machine may end up taking the translators' place.

These and other issues have been being aired ever since MT first reared its head nearly half a century ago. Although patents for translating machines were granted as far back as 1933, the idea of using computers to perform translation is considered to date from a proposal advanced by Warren Weaver, an official of the Rockefeller Foundation, some 15 years later (Weaver 1949). The technology got its first major boost in 1954 in the wake of wide press coverage of the Georgetown-IBM experiment. This two-year project, sponsored by IBM and carried out by Georgetown University in Washington, D.C., culminated in a demonstration on January 7, 1954, in which a set of 49 simple declarative sentences were translated from Russian to English. The experiment showed that the computer could look up vocabulary, recognize the case endings in Russian and provide a preposition or other appropriate equivalent in English, perform minor rearrangement, and make choices between certain words on the basis of syntactic cues (Zarechnak 1979:21-33).

This event was crucial. Far more than the early MT patents and the Warren Weaver proposal, it was the 1954 demonstration and its attendant publicity that gave MT its start in life. What had been a light in the scientists' eyes was now a reality. The event was also a turning-point in that it mobilized the first recruits in what was to be a growing and vocal army of critics who felt that MT was an offense to the genius of language and to the translation profession in particular. And at the same time, it inspired enough optimism and high expectations to launch a sizable government spending spree.

The years since then have witnessed a growing demand for translation in a shrinking world. The translation needs of the U.S. intelligence community, for example, have increased 20-fold since 1960.[1] Over this same period, the international marketing of high-tech products has generated an immense demand for customer support manuals written in fairly simple and repetitive language, required on an urgent basis so that these products can be introduced in multiple markets simultaneously. Today's needs for translation can no longer be met in the context of current budgets and translation costs. As a result, managers look to MT, now quite widely available, as a likely source of help in overcoming the language barrier.

MT has had a checkered career—buffeted, on the one hand, by the telling arguments that have been waged against it and, on the other, by expectations borne of acute need. Despite the ups and downs in its acceptance, however, the product itself has slowly but steadily improved in an ever-growing number of domains and languages. Great strides have been made in syntactic and semantic analysis; some of the pragmatic aspects of language are being addressed; and large quantities of acceptable, or at least fixable, output are being produced and actually used. It is now safe to draw two significant conclusions. The first is that MT is here to stay. The second is that the professional and humanistic issues which it raises are not going to go away.

ATA Addresses the Issues

In 1993 the American Translators Association, concerned about the technology's growing impact on the translation profession, reached out to its 4,500 members in an effort to better understand translators' true concerns, needs, and desires with respect to MT. The purpose of the initiative was to learn which issues were of greatest importance to ATA members and to find out what role translators wanted the Association to play in meeting the challenge. The resulting information will presumably be the basis for a responsive long-term ATA policy in this area.

A questionnaire, developed by the Association's Committee on Machine Translation, was published in the June 1993 issue of the ATA Chronicle.[2] The centerpiece of this poll, and the real focus of the exercise, was a set of 36 statements about machine translation, designed to measure ATA members' attitudes. Each was a commonly heard perception about MT. One-third of the statements were deemed by the developers of the survey to be "negative," one-third were considered "neutral," and one-third were felt to be "positive." The order was scrambled. For each statement, the respondent was asked to check one of six boxes: (1) strongly agree, (2) somewhat agree, (3) neither agree nor disagree, (5) strongly disagree, (4) somewhat disagree, or (6) need more information. Other questions were designed to find out about the respondents' use of computers and their experience with MT as such, as well as to elicit their opinions about various activities and programs which might help to meet their need for more information on the subject.

Unfortunately, the responses had not been compiled and analyzed at the time this book went to press. However, many of the statements in the poll bring to mind the professional issues that translators face. The following sections will refer to some of these issues and discuss the pros and cons as well as the myths and realities. Since the ATA responses were not yet available, in some cases reference has been made to experiences reported in a survey conducted in June 1993 by the International Association for Machine Translation (Vasconcellos 1993a).

Prevailing Impressions

For those who framed the questionnaire, it was easy to draw up a list of prevailing negative attitudes and perceptions about machine translation. Particularly among translators, such impressions abound. It is understandable that translators should have given thought to the issues that MT raises and, even more so, to the translation process itself. After all, translators are the people who really know what translation is about. And for practitioners of the art of translation, it's far easier to imagine why a machine can't do what they do—if not one of the most complex events in the evolution of the cosmos, certainly a formidable task—than to think of ways in which it might share the burden. Regardless of whether they see MT as a threat or a boon, translators are quick to come up with a rich array of reasons why it could have a negative impact on the profession. Although their views tend to be routinely dismissed by others—managers, system developers, translation consumers, the general public—as a latter-day Luddite response, the picture is not that simple. There *are* negatives, even when they are offset by positives. Those who actually use MT may report varying degrees of success—from "the jury is still out" to "indispensable for high-volume jobs" (Vasconcellos 1993a), but common to all of them is a sense that the disadvantages simply have to be accepted because they are outweighed by a series of important benefits to be gained. Always there are tradeoffs, new skills to be learned, and adjustments in the distribution of tasks.

Starting from the recognition, therefore, that "MT is gray"—pluses come with the minuses and vice versa—the following pages will examine some of the impressions most often cited, whether by translators or others. Not surprisingly, at the very head of the list is the Rice Bowl Thing:

- MT WILL TAKE JOBS AWAY FROM TRANSLATORS.

Alas, there is some truth to this statement. To examine the issue fairly, it is important to make a distinction between *existing jobs* and *new work*. As far as existing positions in translation services are concerned, MT does not loom as an imminent threat. The greater danger is that translator posts will fall victim to the worldwide across-the-board trend to replace in-house workers with contractors—in this case, free-lance translators or translation agencies. In most in-house translation services, work volume is growing by leaps and bounds and current resources are thinly stretched. In some cases MT may be introduced, but the increased productivity is more likely to reduce backlogs than to trigger any near-term layoff of staff.

The record shows that there have been a few cases in which MT actually led to a downsizing of in-house translation services. One of these is Environment Canada, which reports[3] that MÉTÉO, the system which translates weather forecasts from English to French and French to English, churns out some 17 million words a year, the equivalent of possibly 30 person-years of traditional translation work, for an all-time total that long since passed the 150-million mark. Up until 1978 translators did this job by hand, of course, and they had to work in shifts around the clock. They quickly got tired of the hours and the monotony, and there was high turnover. Today there are eight translators on staff. MÉTÉO does 85% of the workload; the humans do the other 15% and lightly scan the MT output, changing less than one sentence in 20. While it is true that only a small core of professionals remain on board, and that most of their work is postediting, apparently job satisfaction is greater. Such tasks as building the dictionaries and suggesting changes to the development team relieve the tedium.

It has also been said that the installation of Russian-English SYSTRAN in 1969 at the U.S. Air Force's Foreign Technology Division (now Foreign Aerospace Science and Technology Center—FASTC) resulted in less work for translators of Russian. While there was in fact a decline in the amount of work farmed out, in-house staff strength has remained about the same. According to a manager at FASTC, the drop in contract work is due not so much to MT as it is to a policy decision to discontinue cover-to-cover translation of Russian scientific journals.[4]

The few past cases of downsizing should be viewed in the context of a much larger situation: trends in world politics and the global economy have made for major shifts in the translation market itself. The broader issue that translators need to be addressing is how to reposition themselves in a market dominated by immense volumes of work associated with localization—everything involved in introducing a product or technology in an overseas market, including packaging, procedural guidelines, maintenance instructions, customer support manuals, computer screen displays, and even actual program code. The size of some of these projects boggles the mind: one company turns out 45 million words a year, over half of which is done using MT; another is translating 125 million words over a several-year period, all of it by MT. Work of this kind may well represent the largest demand for translation in the world.[5]

- TRANSLATORS NEED TO BE PREPARED TO DEAL WITH MT.

What happens when MT is introduced in existing in-house translation services is that people are needed for new tasks, principally to collect terminology and feed it into the MT system, as well as sometimes to prepare, or "pre-edit," the input for the machine. Meanwhile, most of the translators continue to translate, some of them postediting MT on-screen. If the decision to adopt MT was the right one and the operation turns out to be successful, some or all of the translators who are postediting will be producing more work, camera-ready, than they did before. These tangible gains in productivity will, in turn, lead managers to consider long-term restructuring.

Of course, everyone involved is learning new skills. This means that sooner or later jobs will get redescribed. Eventually, both for old positions redescribed and for new posts created to fit the changing scene, recruitment will be narrowed to those who have adapted to the new technology. Although there is no substitute for hands-on experience, it is hoped that before too long there will be well-designed courses and thoughtfully prepared training manuals that will help translators to make the transition. While general information can be provided in professional translator publications and in seminars and conferences, the training that is needed is much more detailed.

- POSTEDITING IS DIFFICULT AND TIME-CONSUMING; ANY TRANSLATOR COULD DO THE JOB FASTER FROM SCRATCH. IT IS ALSO BORING AND DEMEANING; THE TRANSLATOR BECOMES A SLAVE TO THE MACHINE.[6]

For sensitive translations and texts that are to be published, it is essential that the machine's output be reviewed by an experienced translator or a technical expert who is proficient in editing and has a good knowledge of the source language. In the case of (1) a highly developed system being used (2) in a restricted domain (3) with a small vocabulary and (4) a limited set of linguistic structures, it may be only a cursory pass and the intervention may be minimal—as with MÉTÉO, for example. But this step cannot be avoided if the client cares about having a correct translation. The posteditor's role becomes even more crucial—and far more challenging—with general translations covering a range of discourse types and subject areas.

There is no question that learning to work with MT output entails a radical adjustment. Postediting is not the same as translating, and not all translators enjoy it. On the other hand, some do. Some become very proficient, increase their productivity, and find that it is less tiring than traditional translation. Often they don't realize how addicted they have become until the machine breaks down or for other reasons they are faced with a translation to do by hand—especially if it is repetitive or has a lot of numbers to copy, pesky format codes to insert, or technical terms to look up. On the other hand, many translators do not take to the process at all. An unfortunate experience at the outset could turn them against MT for good.

There are many reasons why postediting could seem like an overwhelming task. To begin with, the environment could be at fault: the MT system being used could be immature or unsuited to the particular text type; the input text could be poorly written, highly complex in structure, or otherwise inappropriate for MT; or the word processor itself could be cumbersome, without macros to speed up routine maneuvers. There's a degree beyond which trying to fix up the output is no longer worthwhile.

At the same time, the environment isn't everything: the posteditor (who *must* work directly on-screen), should have crackerjack word-processing skills, awareness of postediting strategies, and, above all, a genuine flair for fixing up text. A posteditor of general translations really needs to be a translator-cum-editor. He or she must have the knack of "zapping" a text in just the right places with a minimum of intervention. Some postediting strategies can be learned (Löffler-Laurian 1986, McElhaney and Vasconcellos 1988, Santangelo 1988, Vasconcellos 1985, 1987a, 1989a), but more important is an underlying mind-set which not all translators have. A confidential study conducted in 1986 showed that translators who volunteered to learn MT postediting—all of them experienced and competent professionals—exhibited three basic learning curves: (1) a steep rise at the outset which quickly reached a plateau, (2) a slow and gradual rise that ultimately reached the same level of productivity as the first group, and (3) an essentially flat curve that barely got off the ground. In addition, like regular translators, posteditors must have sufficient knowledge of the subject area and type of discourse to be able to understand the processes being cited and use the right terminology. The level of knowledge required is similar to that of a reviewer or reviser of translations, though the task itself is somewhat different (Vasconcellos 1987b).

This background needs to be understood in order to reach meaningful conclusions about the charges most often leveled against postediting—namely that it's *difficult, time-consuming, boring,* and/or *demeaning.*

The *difficulty* of postediting varies depending on a large number of factors, including the capacity of the MT system, the word processor/macros being used, the nature of the input text, and the word-processing skills, experience, exposure to the domain, MT "training," and mind-set of the person doing the job. To reduce the variables involved, let's assume that the input text is above reproach, the MT system is well developed for the purpose in question, word-processing macros are available, and the translator fills the bill. With simplified or repetitive language or in highly restricted domains, postediting can be easy and quick. With general translations, on the other hand, it can indeed be very difficult—as difficult as traditional translation, with new skills to be learned in addition. For the beginning posteditor, it may take from one to three months of full-time practice before the learning curve reaches a comfortable level. Even at that point, the fact that more work can be produced in less time is deceptive: the brain-twisters are coming up at a faster rate; it needs to be recognized that when the demand for quality is high, the mental effort required for MT postediting is in ways even greater than that needed for traditional translation.

Postediting should not be *time-consuming* if the circumstances are "right"—in other words, if the input text is in the form of an electronic file and if the MT system, the choice of texts, the word processor, the macros, and the posteditor's background and inclinations are in tune with the task. MT users who keep statistics quote productivity increases ranging from 25% to nearly double. In the IAMT study, managers or translators from a total of 18 user sites volunteered positive testimonials about turnaround or productivity. With regard to speed, some of their comments were:[7] "At least 1.8 times better than human-only translation." "Turnaround time is greatly improved." "Turnaround time 6 minutes" [for a weather bulletin]. "Faster turnaround." "Ability to get products to market faster." They also said: "Increases productivity." "40% cost reduction." "Cost savings of nearly 50%." On the other hand, a new user said: "No improvement in speed so far." Elsewhere a freelance translator who has started to use a PC-based system volunteered that she is seeing "a gain of 25%–50% at no extra cost" based on an average daily rate of 5,000 to 6,000 words.[8] If the factors affecting turnaround cannot be adjusted to show a gain over human translation, then it may well be that MT should not be used for the application in question. There is no point in trying to ride a horse that can't get off the ground!

Whether or not postediting is *boring* or *demeaning* will depend on the environment and the perceptions of the individual. Translators may feel less bored or demeaned if they feel positive about the advantages that MT offers. It is interesting to look at the following comments from veteran posteditors, also from the IAMT study: "[It] lightens [my] load." "No cumbersome typing." "Beneficial for us because the kind of text we translate is very dry and repetitive." "I really enjoy working with [this MT system] ... the machine generates a draft translation performing the most boring part of the task so that I can concentrate on perfecting the output." On the other hand, another MT user made the following ambivalent and

118 □ *The Issues of Machine Translation*

thought-provoking comment: "One of the advantages mentioned by salesmen, etc., [namely] that MT relieves translators of boring repetitive tasks, is not relevant in my opinion as there are other repetitive tasks instead: text conversion, parameter editing, deformatting, [etc.] I enjoy working with MT because it is an interesting tool and you learn a lot, but whether it really beats manual translation remains to be seen" (Vasconcellos 1993a).

Postediting should never be imposed to a degree or in a way that results in abusive working conditions for translators. Their "bill of rights" should allow them to always have the option to switch to human translation, with corresponding compensation, whenever they find that a given assignment is unsuitable for MT—and they should be the ones to make this decision. Clearly, if MT increases their productivity by any sizable margin, they should be only too glad to use it.

- MT CONSTRAINS THE CREATIVE USE OF LANGUAGE.

Under appropriate conditions, a clever translator who meets the qualifications described above can use MT output creatively to produce excellent translations (Vasconcellos 1985). The quality of a good postedit is not *necessarily* inferior to that of a good human translation.

Sometimes it is possible to compare the two modes when the same translator uses them both within a single translation job (usually because part of the input text was on a disk and the rest was hard copy). For purposes of argument, it will be assumed that quality is a requirement and that the MT is supposed to mesh seamlessly with the human translation. What appears to happen is that MT produces a quick initial draft, but the draft may need to be rather heavily reviewed in order to give the text a natural flow. The human translation usually takes longer to produce, but it tends to sound more natural.

Often the human translation has a certain *je ne sais quoi*. Élan? Dash? Sparkle? Verve? Vigor? Vitality? Whatever it is, MT doesn't seem to have as much of it. Four of the IAMT respondents (Vasconcellos 1993a) commented on this problem: "It somewhat inhibits creativity." "Loss of idiomacy and style." "Resulting text is a little stilted and awkward." "Excessive adherence to MT output changes expression." This is a factor that should be kept in mind when texts are being selected for machine translation. Perhaps the ideal situation is to provide the translator with MT output and allow him or her to move back and forth, depending on how the translation is coming along, with no reduction in compensation for using MT in the case of freelances.

On the other hand, MT sometimes gets a bum rap. People with strong prejudices may complain about postedited MT without justification. In feedback collected during an 11-month study at the Pan American Health Organization, the end-consumers, who did not know whether or not MT had been used, reported equal satisfaction with both modes; in fact, there were more complaints about traditional human translation (Vasconcellos 1989b).

While there is no inherent reason why a postedited product should sparkle less than a human translation, special precautions may need to be taken. There are times when the posteditor will have to go over the postedit slowly and carefully, or in a separate pass, to smooth out any awkward constructions.

- MT WILL RESULT IN LOWER STANDARDS OF TRANSLATION QUALITY.

The clever translator in the paragraph above also has to be wide awake and working in an environment conducive to maximum concentration. When posteditors get tired or are forced to work amid interruptions, or when there is too much pressure for fast turnaround, quality often suffers. In these circumstances, sometimes the fact that the text is already on the screen can relax the translator's guard too much. It invites complacency. For some strange reason, the screen seems to be more forgiving than hard copy.

In the exercise above, in which the translator is faced with a mixed HT/MT assignment, the first-pass postedit is definitely inferior to the draft human translation. For a quality translation, the postedit needs to be reviewed at least twice again in order to catch the many little lapses that tend to creep in. The human translation is closer to a final, polished product. It can be reviewed more quickly. Machine translation will still be faster, but not by as great a margin as might be expected from the speed of the first pass.

Some of the problems that can occur when the posteditor is under pressure include: portions of the text left unseen, word-processing errors, awkward passages, misconstructions of the original meaning (usually due to insufficient checking against the original text), failure to detect blatant mistranslations, an incorrect name of an important entity or institution, a garbled proper name, etc. In some cases an oversight can be quite serious. The translation consumer relies on the accuracy of postedited MT (whereas raw MT, clearly labeled, makes no promises).

When translation quality is a priority, it is important for the translator to be aware of the risk of lapses and try to prevent them by staying refreshed, minimizing interruptions, and planning ahead, insofar as possible, to avoid last-minute rushes. It is also essential that the postedit be double-checked, including at least one review on hard copy.

Standards of translation quality will decline as long as sloppiness, whether generated by the machine or the human, is tolerated.

Raw, unpostedited MT should not be a threat to translation standards. It is not intended to replace translation and can be used for purposes that are beyond human capacity in terms of speed, volume, and reduced cost. It should be recognized that sometimes a picture-perfect translation is unnecessary. MT is assuming an increasingly important role as a processor or "information-only" drafts. Some users—for example, most of the 1,600-plus analysts served by FASTC at Wright-Patterson Air Force Base, who plug into MT on-line, are willing to settle for unpostedited raw output (Vasconcellos and Bostad 1992). In a study conducted at Sandia National Laboratories, 34 of 41 analysts found raw MT output acceptable for their purposes (Newman 1988). At the European Commission, 70% of the 30 million words of MT churned out annually is for immediate use by managers and others outside the translation services.[9]

Part of this information-only volume may be for spotting texts that need to be fully translated. Several of the respondents in the IAMT survey reported that they use MT for triage, to decide whether or not to send a job out for a full translation. In the end, the proliferation of raw MT should underscore the importance of human translators, and generate more assignments for them, because the distinction between the machine output and what a person can do will become patently clear to all.

- MT WILL CONTRIBUTE TO THE PUBLIC'S POOR UNDERSTANDING OF THE TRANSLATION PROCESS; TRANSLATION CONSUMERS WILL EXPECT MIRACLES.

Nontranslators are largely unaware of the translation process and the complexity that it entails. Unfortunately, the widespread availability of MT for personal computers has raised unrealistic expectations in the public mind. Many people who need quality translations turn to MT in the hope that it will spare them the cost of a proper professional product. This kind of thinking does a great disservice to the profession. It may well be MT's darkest legacy.

Translators need to join forces in an unrelenting effort to inform the public about the real nature of translation. However, such a campaign must be credible. It needs to take into account the role that MT can play, rather than denounce it, especially with inaccurate claims and statements. A shrill attack against MT is often perceived by people outside the profession as a defense of vested interests and outmoded working methods, and as such it tends to be discredited.

- MT IS BEING USED BY PEOPLE WHO DON'T KNOW MUCH ABOUT TRANSLATION.

It is true that more and more people outside the profession are getting involved in translation. While MT is contributing to the trend, the underlying cause is the mammoth growth in localization. This relatively recent development, even though it means that more translation is being done in the world, has a down side for translators, for it has meant that MT is being used increasingly by nontranslators and that in some cases decisions are being made by managers who lack knowledge about the translation process and may not be able to judge the product they're getting. As the translation market gravitates toward areas in which profit margins are tighter and speed of delivery makes a big difference in the bottom line, managers are driven to look for economies wherever they can find them, and MT becomes very attractive. It promises a fully automated publishing chain with large savings in the porting of formats, accurate carryover of numerals and formulas, uniform terminology, and faster turnaround, to mention a few advantages. In addition, postediting is typically compensated at lower rates than full translation—from *really* low rates up to a maximum of about 70%—and nontranslators are willing settle for less. Moreover, they are eager to give it a try, whereas regular translators don't always want to do this kind of work; they would rather not devote their career to a project involving, say, 100,000 pages about the innards of a telephone switching system (a true case in point). As a result, recruitment is increasingly directed outside the translation profession. And because translators are often absent from this market, the agencies that do employ them may find themselves at a disadvantage when they try to bid for jobs.

At the same time, it is safe to assume that good, experienced professionals will always play a major role wherever sensitive translations are needed—translations that will be closely scrutinized or published and read by a large audience.

• MT PRODUCTS ARE CONFUSING; PRICES RANGE FROM 80 TO 50 TIMES THAT MUCH.

MT products *are* confusing. It is beyond the scope of this essay to explain the differences between the various types of MT systems and platforms,[10] but with any system the translator needs to bear in mind a basic set of principles which ensure that its use is maximized.

Since MT is not always cost-effective, independent translators should approach it with caution. It involves an up-front investment to buy the software, and sometimes the hardware, and to build up the dictionary to meet the user's own requirements, which may take from three to six months (Vasconcellos 1993b). These investments will be justified if costs can be trimmed over the long term. Much will depend on having a large and steady volume of input text (probably at least 100,000 words a month) that is straightforward in style with a minimum of ambiguity and preferably in a single domain. The other conditions described in the preceding sections are also essential. Barbara Thomas, the freelance medical translator who achieves productivity increases of 25% to 50%, sums it up: All MT programs present the translator with similar problems: (1) the original must be not only machine-readable but well-written and checked for spelling and grammar; (2) the skills for postediting MT output must be developed; postediting requires a great deal of mental effort; and (3) don't count on enormous increases in productivity overnight.

Conclusion

Appreciating MT is a question of balancing the pros and cons and the pluses and minuses. If the arguments above have seemed contradictory and confusing, it's because they are. Even veteran users get confused. There are many variables to examine, juggle, and trade off, and the variables themselves are fraught with conditions, complexities, and inconsistencies. In the whole picture, perhaps only one conclusion can be reached without qualification: MT is here to stay.

The professional associations have an obligation to provide the briefings and detailed training that will help translators adjust to working with MT, and it is up to translators themselves to take an active role in implementing it so that it leads the profession forward rather than into dark alleys and up dead-end streets.

NOTES

[1] In 1960, at hearings before the Special Investigating Subcommittee of the Committee on Science and Astronautics of the U. S. House of Representatives, John J. Bagnall of the Central Intelligence Agency testified that the Russian output of scientific information was 780 million words a year, 53 million (7%) of which was being translated by the intelligence community. In 1993, according to speakers at the Symposium on Advanced Information Processing and Analysis (2-4 March), the intelligence community faced the challenge of sifting through a volume of 150 billion words, now in a variety of different languages.

[2] Respondents were asked to provide their ATA membership number, a requirement which effectively limited coverage to ATA members and at the same time precluded duplicate returns from any one individual.

[3] Information provided directly by Environment Canada in Response to IAMT survey (results published in Vasconellos 1993).

[4] Dale A. Bostad, FASTC, personal communication, January 1993.

[5] In the IAMT study, 23 users reported their annual MT translation volume: together, they produce 170 million words a year, and of this total volume, 108 million, or 64%, is for localization. It is interesting to note, by the way, that of the total study population of 40 MT users, 80% started to use MT in the last five years. (All data from Vasconcellos 1993.)

[6] The author, formerly the chief of translation and terminology at the Pan American Health Organization in Washington, D.C., speaks with authority on this issue, having postedited several million words of machine translation in a large range of subject areas over a period of 14 years and having worked with over 50 posteditors.

[7] Responses received in the IAMT study, including some not reported in Vasconcellos 1993.

[8] From a CompuServe thread, August 1993.

[9] Response received in the IAMT study.

[10] Summary information on PC-based MT systems is available from ATA Headquarters (1735 Jefferson Davis Highway, Suite 903, Arlington, Virginia 22202-3413). *Byte* magazine had a state-of-the-art section on MT for PCs and workstations in January 1993 (see especially "Babelware for the Desktop" by L. Chris Miller). For more technical background on MT systems, see Hutchins (1986), Hutchins and Somers (1992), Vasconcellos (in press). The Association for Machine Translation in the Americas (655 Fifteenth Street, N.W., Suite 310, Washington, D.C. 20005) provides a bibliography on the practical use of MT.

REFERENCES

Hutchins, W. J. *Machine Translation: Past, Present, Future.* New York: Wiley & Sons, 1986.
Hutchins, W. John, and Harold L. Somers. *An Introduction to Machine Translation.* New York, etc.: Academic Press, 1992.
Löffler-Laurian, Anne-Marie. "Post-édition rapide et post-édition conventionelle." Part 1, *Multilingua* 5 (1986): 81-88; part 2, 5: 225-29.
McElhaney, Terrence, and Muriel Vasconcellos. "The Translator and the Postediting Experience." Muriel Vasconcellos, ed. *Technology as Translation Strategy,* American Translators Association Series, Vol. 2. New York: SUNY-Binghamton Press, 1988. 140-48.
Miller, L. Chris. "Babelware for the Desktop." and "Resource Guide." *Byte* Jan (1993): 177-83 and 185-86.
Mitamura, Teruko, Eric H. Nyberg, 3rd, and Jaime G. Carbonell. "Automated Corpus Analysis and the Acquisition of Large, Multi-lingual Knowledge Bases for MT." *Proceedings of the Fifth International Conference on Theoretical and Methodological Issues in Machine Translation.* Kyoto, 14-16 July 1993. 312-28.
Newman, Patricia E. "Information-Only Machine Translation: A Feasibility Study." Muriel Vasconcellos, ed. *Technology as Translation Strategy,* American Translators Association Series, Vol. 2. New York: SUNY-Binghamton Press, 1988. 178-89.
Richards, I. "Toward a Theory of Translation." American Anthropological Association, ed. *Studies in Chinese Thought,* Vol. 55, memoir 75. Chicago: Univ. of Chicago Press, 1953.
Santangelo, Susana. "Making an MT System Work: Perspective of a Translator." Muriel Vasconcellos, ed. *Technology as Translation Strategy,* American Translators Association Series, Vol. 2. New York: SUNY-Binghamton Press, 1988. 133-39.
Schütz, Jörg, and Bärbel Ripplinger. "Machine Translation Supported by Terminological Information." *Proceedings of the Fifth International Conference on Theoretical and Methodological Issues in Machine Translation.* Kyoto, 14-16 July 1993. 102-16.
Vasconcellos, Muriel. "Functional Considerations in the Postediting of Machine-Translated Output." *Computers and Translation* 1 (1985): 21-38.
———. "Postediting On-screen: Machine Translation from Spanish into English." *A Profession on the Move: Translating and the Computer 8.* Ed. Catriona Picken. London: Aslib, 1987. 133-46.
———. "A Comparison of MT Postediting and Traditional Revision." *Across the Language Gap: Proceedings of the 28th Annual Conference of the American Translators Association.* Karl Kummer, ed. Albuquerque, 8-11 October 1987. Medford, NJ: Learned Information, 1987. 409-16.
———. "Cohesion and Coherence in the Presentation of Machine Translation Products." *Georgetown University Round Table on Languages and Linguistics 1989.* Washington, D.C.: Georgetown Univ. Press, 1989. 89-105.
———. "Long-Term Data for an MT Policy." *Literary and Linguistic Computing* 4.3 (1989): 203-13.
———. "The Present State of Machine Translation Usage Technology, Or: How Do I Use Thee? Let Me Count the Ways." *International Cooperation for Global Communication: Proc MT Summit IV.* Kobe, 19-22 July 1993. 35-46.

———. "Is MT Right for You?" *Byte* Jan (1993): 180.
———. "Terminology and Machine Translation." *Handbook of Terminology Management*. Ed. Sue Ellen Wright and Gerhard Budin. Amsterdam: John Benjamins, in press.
Vasconcellos, Muriel, and Dale A. Bostad. "Machine Translation in a High-Volume Translation Environment." *Computers in Translation: A Practical Appraisal*. Ed. John Newton. London and New York: Routledge, 1992. 58–77.
Weaver, Warren. "Translation." Rpt. in *Machine Translation of Languages*. Ed. W. N. Locke and A. D. Booth. Cambridge, MA: MIT Press, 1955.
Zarechnak, Michael. "The History of Machine Translation." *Machine Translation*. Ed. Bozena Henisz-Dostert, R. Ross Macdonald, and Michael Zarechnak. The Hague: Mouton, 1979.

The Translator Workstation

ALAN K. MELBY

     Over the past 10 years, the issue of whether or not a translator should use a computer has largely been replaced by the issue of what kind of computer hardware and software to acquire in order to best succeed in the translation market. This shift implies that computers are generally assumed to be useful to the translator. This article will use "translator workstation" to describe the hardware/software system used by a translator. The hardware exists only to support the software. The software, in turn, exists only to serve the translator. This article will emphasize three ways in which a translator workstation can serve the translator: (1) allowing the translator to effectively serve remote clients through electronic transmission of text, (2) assisting the translator in maintaining high-quality translations through consistent use of terminology, and (3) permitting efficient document production through electronic information retrieval and integration with the rest of the document production path. Translators should consider at least these three points when acquiring or upgrading a translator workstation.

    This article distinguishes three components of a translator workstation: (a) the hardware, (b) the operating environment, and (c) the application software. It also illustrates what a translator workstation is, and explains the three-level model that is used to describe translator workstations.

1. Some Definitions

1.1 HARDWARE

The hardware consists of physical components, such as the power supply, the case, the monitor, the hard disk, the diskette drives, and the keyboard.

1.2 OPERATING ENVIRONMENT

The operating environment interacts directly with the hardware. It consists of the operating system and the user interface. On a Macintosh, the standard operating environment (such as System 7) integrates the operating system and user interface very tightly. On a PC, the most common operating system is MS-DOS™. Until recently, the most common initial user-interface was the DOS prompt (e.g., "C:\>") or one of the many menu systems that hide the DOS prompt from the user. Now MS-Windows™ is becoming the most common user interface for PCs. Windows version 3.1 is a separate program that runs on top of DOS. "Chicago" is the Microsoft code name for a new version of Windows that will integrate DOS and Windows, forming an operating environment somewhat similar to the Macintosh operating environment.

1.3 APPLICATION SOFTWARE

The application software consists of packages designed to perform specific tasks for the user. For a translator, typical application software would be a word processor, a telecommunications package, and an accounting system.

1.4 WORKBENCH, PLATFORM, WORKSTATION

Sometimes people mention a "writer's workbench" or a "translator's workbench." These terms generally refer to a set of application software packages that function together in a given operating environment. They do not include the hardware or the operating environment itself, as does the term "translator workstation." You also hear about "platforms," which generally include various hardware together with a single operating environment but not including application software. As we will use it in this article, a translator workstation is a *complete* hardware/software system, including a platform and applications software, ready for the translator to begin the work of translation. The term workstation, when used alone, usually refers to a powerful computer with high resolution graphics capabilities, often running the Unix™ operating system.

1.5 THREE-LEVEL DESIGN

This paper examines the translator workstation in terms of a three-level design. The first level translator workstation applies when the source text is on paper; the second level applies when the source text is on diskette (or in some other electronic form); and the third level applies when machine translation is used.

This article does not attempt to treat machine translation in detail. It does, however, overview the current and future possibilities of the translator workstation. It also gives general guidelines for translators planning to acquire a computer and suggests what components can be added to a minimal translator workstation to improve its effectiveness in the hands of the translator. A minimal translator workstation is a PC or Macintosh with a word processor. But that is only the beginning.

A complete three-level translator workstation is a harmonious combination of hardware, operating environment, and application software. In the rest of this article, we will first describe the major hardware components that should be included in a translator workstation; then we will briefly discuss the major operating environments among which a translator must choose. Finally, we will discuss the three levels of the application software for a translator workstation.

2. *Hardware Components*

2.1 THE SYSTEM UNIT

The system unit is enclosed in a case that contains the power supply and the central processing unit (CPU), which is generally mounted on a motherboard along with the memory (RAM). The "bus" allows "cards" to be attached to the motherboard. Generally, the system unit will also include a hard disk drive and one or more diskette drives.

2.2 PERIPHERALS

Peripherals are components that are not usually part of the system unit. The most basic peripherals are the keyboard and the video display unit (VDU). In addition, most computers now come with a "mouse" or other pointing device. In some cases a system unit, a monitor, a keyboard, and even a pointing device can be built into a single physical unit, blurring the distinction between central and peripheral components. In a strict historical sense, however, everything but the central processor and RAM is peripheral.

Nearly every translator adds a printer as a peripheral component, and many translators now have a modem for sending and receiving data over telephone lines. In addition, most translators have a fax capability, either as a stand-alone unit or as a "fax/modem" card attached to the bus of the system unit.

The technology used in scanners (devices that scan a page and produce a computer file "picture" of it made of tiny dots), stand-alone fax machines, modems, printers and photocopiers is highly related. For example, a stand-alone fax machine can be thought of as a special-purpose computer with a built-in scanner, modem and printer. It is therefore no surprise that we are beginning to see such combinations as printers that can also be used to receive faxes and photocopiers that can be used as scanners. Within a few years we can logically expect to see a single device serving as a combined printer, photocopier, fax machine, modem, and scanner, when connected to your computer. For the moment, however, the situation is somewhat unstable. It typically causes a duplication of similar hardware (i.e., a laser printer and a photocopier sitting side by side).

Optical Character Recognition (OCR) is an additional technology, requiring a scanner and an application software package. OCR software converts the scanned image of a page of text (which is just dots and cannot be edited with a word processor) to a word processing file (which *can* be edited with a word processor). The problem with OCR technology is that it makes recognition errors, perhaps interpreting an 'r' plus an 'i' as an 'n'. An error rate of less than two percent is hard to obtain, yet may still be too high to make OCR useful for translators.

An important (but often omitted) component of a translator's system is a backup device such as a tape drive. Terminology and word processing files are generally saved on a hard disk. But hard disks are not infallible, and many translators lose much time (and therefore money) because they do not back up their files—when their hard disk fails, their most important files become inaccessible. The only way to prevent such a disaster is to back up files often (usually daily, so you can lose no more than one day's work). There are two ways to do backup: (a) back up an entire hard disk (sometimes called a complete backup), or (b) back up just the files that have been modified since the last backup (sometimes called an incremental backup). An incremental backup does not require any special hardware—you can use the diskette drive that is found in every system unit. But you do need an application software package (or operating system utility) designed to allow incremental backup. A complete backup can be done using [many, many] diskettes, but this method of doing a complete backup is cumbersome, slow and irritating at best. For complete backups, we suggest a tape drive using a tape cartridge. Tape drives for backup are becoming much more affordable, often adding less than ten percent to the cost of a total computer system.

Another component which is becoming less expensive is a CD-ROM drive. A CD-ROM has the same physical dimensions as an audio compact disk (CD), but it is used to store computer data (about six hundred megabytes of it per CD-ROM!). The Canadian government's terminology database (Termium™) is now available on CD-ROM, and other databases useful to translators will become available in the future.

And in some circumstances, e.g., when large amounts of data must be transmitted by mail in an easily accessible form, a removable cartridge disk drive is needed. A 3 1/2" diskette is easily removable (unlike your hard disk), but the term "removable cartridge drive" is usually reserved for drives that accept high-capacity cartridges. In 1994, a typical removable cartridge disk holds up to 150 megabytes of data. Removable disks are more expensive than tape cartridges, but they are also more flexible. With a removable disk, you can copy or edit any file instantly, as you can on a hard disk; however, with a tape cartridge, you can only read or write sequentially from the beginning of the tape to the end.

2.3 SELECTING A SYSTEM UNIT AND PERIPHERALS

Since microcomputer technology changes so rapidly, it is difficult to give any specific suggestions that will still be valid six months in the future. However, to avoid stopping with only a frustrating list of options, we will make some suggestions about how a translator might select a computer. Understand that such suggestions should be shown to a knowledgeable friend who can add up-to-the-minute information.

If you are buying a new computer in early 1994, the first decision to make is whether to (a) enter the world of Apple computer, or (b) enter the world of the IBM-PC compatible. If you choose option (a) you buy a Macintosh™, sometimes called a "Mac." If you choose (b) you purchase a "PC" from IBM, or from one of the many other vendors whose microcomputers run the same software as an IBM PS/2. This decision between a Mac and a PC is like a fork in the road: everything is different from then on. Even though there is a package that allows some PC software to run on a Mac, it runs so slowly that most people are not satisfied. In general, there are "Mac people" and "PC people" but few who are really comfortable in both worlds.

A recent development is that IBM, Apple, and Motorola have teamed up to create the PowerPC CPU chip. Apple will produce PowerMacs based on the PowerPC chip. IBM will produce Power Personal Systems, also based on the PowerPC chip. This will allow a further merging of the Mac and PC worlds. Until the PowerPC chip, all Macs used chips made by Motorola in a series with code numbers of the form 680x0 and all PCs used chips from Intel in a series with numbers of the form 80x86 or the trademark Pentium. Eventually, you should be able to run some version of the Mac operating environment and some version of Windows both on the same computer, without either one being run in "emulation" mode (which slows down performance considerably).

We cannot tell you whether the Mac or the PC world is better, but almost anyone you ask will have a strong opinion one way or the other. We can, however, report that in a recent survey, over 90 percent of those ATA members responding use a computer. Of the computer users, about 15 percent use a Mac while about 85 percent use some type of IBM PC compatible (Childs and Penthrodokous, Proceedings of 1991 ATA Conference, © 1991 Learned Information).

Whichever way you go, here are some basic questions to ask before purchasing a new computer:

(a) Is the system expandable? Even if you start out with a minimal system, choose a system with the following features:

- Mac: - a "superdrive" that can read DOS diskettes
  - a motherboard that can accept at least eight Meg of RAM
  - a CPU with at least the power of an LC model Mac

- PC: - a 3 1/2 inch 1.44 Meg diskette drive
  - a 5 1/4 inch 1.2 Meg diskette drive

- a VGA-resolution screen (or higher)
- a motherboard that can accept at least eight Meg of RAM
- a CPU with at least the power of an Intel 486 33 Mhz

- both:
  - a hard disk that holds at least 80 Meg
  - room to add a second hard disk later
  - a mouse or other pointing device
  - a printer or an option to add one later
  - a modem or an option to add one later
  - a tape drive or room to add one later
  - a CD-ROM drive or room to add one later

An apparent exception to the above specifications would be the case of a local area network (LAN) in which one printer or one CD-ROM is shared among several users. In this case, you may have a "virtual" or "network" printer or other shared peripheral.

Until fax/modem cards improve or until combination printer/fax/modem/copier/scanner units become available and affordable, one flexible and fairly low-cost solution for an individual translator is to purchase an inexpensive laser printer, an inexpensive thermal or plain-paper fax machine, an external modem (with lights that tell the status—useful in solving problems) or an internal modem with software that tells you the status, and an inexpensive personal copier. Then, over the next few years, some of those functions can be combined into fewer components. Meanwhile faxes can be sent by printing them out and faxing them (providing a paper record of what was sent) and important faxes can be archived by copying them. An unresolved problem with fax/modem cards is that they are still not as trouble-free in communicating with a variety of other fax machines and modems as stand-alone fax machines and external modems with status lights. Beware of advertising claims to the contrary. Of course, all this will change over the years.

(b) Is the system serviceable? Whom do you call if the system stops working? Do they provide on-site service? Do you have to carry in the system? Do you have to mail in the system? Do they provide a replacement system while you are waiting for repairs? Are parts and/or labor included in a warranty? For how many months?

(c) Will the system handle the target languages I work with?

This question is a hard one because the typical computer store sales representative will not be able to answer it. The same sales representative who seems very knowledgeable in answering questions about specifications of "hardware components" and "service" may suddenly seem totally ignorant if asked whether the proposed system can handle Russian.

Our suggestion concerning the important topic of language support is to check with a colleague who translates into the language in question. Ask what computer hardware, operating environment, and applications software he or she uses for that language. Find out specifically which computer, video display unit, operating environment, printer, word processor, and (if applicable) terminology management software and desktop publishing software he or she uses, since these components must work together to support the language in question. Then give this information to the computer sales representative in writing as part of your requirements, rather than just saying that you want a computer that can do language X.

Obviously your choice of hardware components cannot be made independently of your choice of operating environment and applications software. Everything must work together. Many people actually start with the applications software they want to use and choose hardware and an operating environment that will support it.

3. Operating Environments

At present, your choice of operating environments is severely constrained by your choice of hardware. In the future, as previously mentioned, there will be operating systems that will run identically on several different kinds of hardware. Some may object to this statement, claiming that the Unix™ operating system already meets this criterion, but we reply that the "minor" differences between different versions of Unix create major difficulties in trying to run the same applications software on different kinds of computers.

As of early 1994, there were three practical platforms for an individual translator: straight MS-DOS (DOS for short), DOS+Windows (Windows for short), and Mac (meaning the standard Apple operating system for the Macintosh). The choice between DOS, Windows, and Mac is not an easy one. Most people believe that DOS will largely disappear within five years, having been replaced by Windows (including Windows NT, which does not require DOS), but in 1994, DOS is still a viable platform and has the following advantage. If you are on a very tight budget and even the "minimal" system suggested above is too expensive, an "AT" class PC with

DOS and WordPerfect can be purchased for less than one thousand dollars. Such "subminimal" systems can be used for translation into English, French, or German (and several other Western European languages) without additional hardware (except perhaps a printer and modem).

However, Windows and Mac are generally expected to be the dominant platforms by 1995. These platforms both include Graphical User Interfaces (GUIs) and are more similar to each other than either is to DOS. At least operating environments are becoming more similar rather than less.

Other operating environments being pushed very hard at present are OS/2 and Unix. These are important operating environments for some users, but probably not for translators, at least individual translators. Unix is fundamentally a multi-user operating system (that is, it supports several users on the same computer at the same time). IBM owns and develops OS/2. Novell has purchased the Unix trademark as well as acquiring WordPerfect Corporation. This suggests that Microsoft, IBM, and Novell/WordPerfect be watched carefully for developments.

However, for most translators, the question boils down to the unanswerable choice between the PC world (which implies DOS or Windows now and later Windows) and the Mac world (which implies the Mac operating environment).

4. Application Software—Three-level Design

Application software for a translator workstation can be categorized into three levels. Although this three-level design was first presented over ten years ago (Melby, 1982, "Proceedings of the 1982 Coling Conference in Prague"), it has weathered well, despite amazing advances in microcomputer hardware and software.

4.1 Level One

Level one consists of those translator tools (application software packages) that can be used when the source text is on paper. They start with a word processor, which is used to enter the target text into a computer file. Practically no one uses a typewriter for translation anymore—even dictating translators have secretaries who use word processors. Around the word processor, there are a number of useful utilities, such as a spell checker, a thesaurus, and a billing system. The billing system may be as simple as a word count from the spell checker, or it may be a specialized billing package for translators, which gives more control over the way words are counted and partially automates the production of an invoice. Of course, a general accounting system is useful to an individual translator or a service bureau but is not considered a translator tool and so is not discussed here.

Word Processing Utilities and Related Software

One utility that is very useful when more than one person edits a file (i.e., in the case of a translator/revisor team) is a file comparison program that finds and highlights differences between two versions of a document.

Clients often require a document to be delivered in a certain word processor format. In this case, when the required format is not that of your word processor, a file format conversion utility can be essential.

Sometimes a client will ask the translator to produce camera-ready copy, which means the translator takes on the additional role of "typesetter" and may require the translator to use a desktop publishing (DTP) software package tied to the word processor.

An additional utility that can be very useful is a search program that will look for key words within a potentially large set of word processing files. This comes in handy when there is a large data base of previously translated documents and a certain document must be retrieved, but the file name of the document is not known. In that case, a search program can look for key words in a large set of documents and tell the translator which documents contain those words, thus speeding up the retrieval process.

Many of these features (spell check, thesaurus, word count, creation of forms such as invoices, file comparison, file format conversion, and search across more than one document) are already built into word processors or soon will be. In the meantime, or when a built-in feature is not satisfactory, add-on utilities can be purchased that will work with the popular word processors. The two DOS word processors with the most market share are WordPerfect™ and Microsoft Word™. In the Windows world, the Ami™ word processor also draws a substantial market share. But these general market share facts become relatively unimportant if a given word processor will not support the language you translate into. In that case, you may be forced to use a less-known word processor that supports your target language, particularly if that language uses Arabic script or belongs to the CJK family (Chinese, Japanese, and Korean).

Many translators have heard about Unicode and wonder about its significance. Unicode is a character set that uses 16 bits per character instead of the usual 8 bits. What this means is that there are over 60,000 potential characters in Unicode, while there are only 256 in any one eight-bit character set. Eventually, there will be operating environments and word processors for both Macs and PCs that will fully support Unicode. That will mean that many languages can be mixed in a single word processing document, including Roman alphabet languages, Cyrillic, Arabic, and Greek alphabet languages, as well as Chinese, Japanese, and Korean. But this power will come at a price: huge amounts of disk space will be required to hold even one complete Unicode font. However, for many individuals and organizations, the advantage of allowing all their languages to be combined in one document will be well worth the price.

Telecommunications Software

Another component of the level-one translator workstation is telecommunications software. This is software that makes a modem useful. The simplest telecommunications software is a terminal emulator. Terminal emulation software may come with your modem or can usually be purchased from the same source. One commonly used terminal emulator is called Procomm and is available as shareware. Some of the common tasks for which translators employ modems are to transfer files electronically, to send electronic mail (e-mail) messages to colleagues (and receive them), and to consult electronic "bulletin boards" and other on-line services.

The most important difference between sending a word processing file by fax vs. modem is that a fax cannot be immediately edited and reprinted (or printed on a laser printer for high quality copy) on the receiving end; it must first be converted to a word-processing file. In contrast, a file that is transferred by modem can be edited on the receiving end, assuming that the receiver has either a compatible word processor or a conversion program to make the file compatible. There has been some discussion of a combination between fax and modem transfer in which a document is faxed and then converted at the receiving end into a disk file using OCR (optical character recognition). Unfortunately, this method introduces too many errors using current fax transmission methods.

One warning to translators: word processing documents should not be sent by regular e-mail. This will usually result in the loss of format information and/or the loss of accented characters. Word processing files should be sent over telephone lines using the following method:

First, compress the file using one of the common utilities available for this purpose (in the DOS/Windows world, the most common utility of this type is called PKZIP). Then transmit the file using a "protocol" that includes error detection and correction. The most common (although not most sophisticated) protocol used by telecommunication software packages is called XMODEM. This will allow the detection and correction of errors caused by noise on the telephone lines. If you are not certain the receiver has the corresponding decompression utility, transmit it too.

This transfer method has several advantages. At the other end the file can be decompressed, edited and printed as if you had delivered a copy of the word processing file on diskette. The compression/transfer/decompression process reduces transfer time, thus reducing the transfer cost, and produces on the other end a file of exactly the same size and date as the original. It also adds an additional assurance that the file was transmitted accurately, since a garbled file will produce an error message when the receiver tries to decompress it.

The significance of file transfer is, of course, that it allows a team to work closely together without being physically in the same building or even the same city. For an individual translator, experience in electronic file transfer can make the difference in getting a particular contract or not, since a client may not be willing to wait for files to be sent by mail on diskette. And the old-fashioned practice of retyping a translation delivered by fax should soon disappear. It is inefficient, unnecessarily expensive, and error-prone.

For an in-house translator in a large organization, file transfer allows the entire document production path—from authoring to translating to review to final printing—to be integrated without retyping anything and without shipping delays, even if the document production path spans several continents.

One form of file transfer is direct transfer. In this form, both parties must be actively involved in the process at the same time. One side waits in "auto answer" mode for the other side to place a telephone call which establishes a connection. A second method is to use a private electronic BBS (Bulletin Board System). If you have an extra computer, even an old "XT" class PC (which can be purchased used for a few hundred dollars), you can set up your own BBS which stands ready at all times to receive a file while you do other things. You can also place a file on your BBS and send a fax or e-mail message to notify the other party that the file is ready to be picked up. With a BBS, your clients can place a file on your BBS at any time (even during the night) and you can pick it up at your convenience. And your client can pick up a file at their convenience, even if you are not available at the time. This is especially useful for file transfers that cross many time zones. One problem to overcome is that the modem on your BBS must always be connected to a phone line to receive calls. This requires either a dedicated phone line for the BBS or a "switch box" that can detect the difference between voice, fax, and modem calls and connect the line to the appropriate device (your BBS modem, your fax machine, or your telephone). If you already have a dedicated fax line, then a switch box can route calls on that line to the fax or BBS.

A third method of file transfer is to use an on-line service, such as CompuServe. Both sender and receiver should subscribe to the same on-line service. Then the sender transmits a word-processing file in binary mode. Again, do not send a word processing file as an e-mail message in text mode. Even though there are "gateways" between various on-line services, they may not support binary file transfer. The ATA Translation and Computers Committee has suggested (in 1993) using CompuServe when there is a choice. Internet, which is receiving much publicity, is not exactly an on-line service, but rather a collection of linked computers that can be accessed through various on-line services. CompuServe already provides limited access to the Internet for e-mail messages in text mode. CompuServe support for binary file transfer through the Internet should become available.

Once you have the basic hardware and software necessary to perform an electronic file transfer, many other possibilities open up. One important task in sci-tech translation is terminology research. When an equivalent is not supplied by the requester of the translation and is not found by the translator upon consulting bilingual lexical/terminological resources in the office (such as technical dictionaries on paper and in electronic form), there are two methods normally used to find the term: (1) consult a colleague or (2) find a target language document which treats the same subject matter topic as the source text. Your modem can assist you with both approaches.

Using a commercial on-line service such as Compuserve, you can send an e-mail message to a colleague without using your telephone. E-mail works only when you and your colleague both check your electronic "mailbox" regularly and use the same on-line service, but when these conditions are met, e-mail is better than telephone calls for three reasons: (1)

you do not risk interrupting your colleague at a busy moment, as you do with a phone call, (2) e-mail messages are generally less expensive than phone calls, and (3) you can send a question which can be looked at by all the members of a special interest group (SIG). These first two advantages also apply to asking questions by fax, but only e-mail offers the third feature. Compuserve has a SIG for those interested in foreign languages, FLEFLO. FLEFLO can be used by translators to post questions about terminology. For example, you might ask if anyone knows the Norwegian term for ABS (anti-lock braking system). Someone you do not even know might browse through the questions that have been posted and send you the answer electronically. With large-scale electronic networks and a spirit of cooperation, it is almost as if individuals with common interests live in the same village, even though they are scattered around the world.

If you cannot find a colleague with the answer to your terminology question, you may resort to studying relevant documents written in the target language to find appropriate terms. A modem may even be able to help you find relevant documents. On-line services for locating documents are usually available at large libraries, especially university libraries. They use modems to connect with bibliographic databases such as Dialog. Sometimes you can even arrange access to a library's electronic card catalog from your computer by modem, saving unnecessary travel time to library when the library does not have what is needed.

The March 15, 1994, issue of *PC Magazine* (Vol. 13, No. 5) featured on-line services and is a good source of additional information.

Terminology Management

Another important component of level one besides telecommunication for e-mail, file transfer, and terminology research, is terminology management. Every sci-tech translator must somehow manage the terminology associated with the domain or domains into which documents are translated. Once a good equivalent is found for a technical term, it should be stored away for future use, to avoid having to do the research all over again. See Wright ("The Role of Terminology in Translation-oriented Quality Assurance" in the proceedings of the 1991 ATA conference) for a discussion of the importance of managing translation-oriented terminology files with a record for each concept (not just one-to-one glossaries).

There are basically three ways to manage terminology: in your head, on some form of paper or cardstock, or electronically. With the number of new terms growing so dramatically, few people can retrieve them accurately from their head, except perhaps in the case where a translator deals regularly with many documents in one narrow domain. The traditional form of paper-based terminology management is to store terms on index cards and to retrieve information by manually searching through boxes of cards. The new way to manage terminology is to store it on disk and retrieve it using a terminology management software package. An intermediate method is to store terminological data in a standard word processing document and retrieve it using standard word processing commands. This intermediate method is simple to set up but is inherently limited in its possibilities. The solution with the greatest potential for powerful management of terminology is specialized software.

Several commercial software packages have been designed to assist the translator in managing terminology files. When selecting a package you should keep in mind the objectives of terminology management, including flexibility, consistency, and efficiency. We will discuss each of these three objectives.

A terminology management system must be flexible enough to allow information to be recorded in a natural way. Some terms will have multiple target language equivalents, depending on the subject matter domain or a client's preference within a domain. Some will have long definitions and several notes. Some will require relatively little information. An index card system allows for flexibility by allowing a piece of information, such as a definition or a contextual example, to take a part of a line or several lines. In a computer file, such a piece of information would be called a "field." And one entry can span several cards if needed. In a concept-oriented database, there will probably be a separate card for use of a term, for example, "hub" as in a component of an automobile tire and "hub" as in a computer hardware component of the wiring of a local area network. A traditional database system with fixed length keys and fixed length records of fixed length fields is not well-suited for terminology management. Therefore, a terminology management system should allow for varying length keys and data. It should also be flexible enough to allow access to your own entries (that is, entries you have created yourself), entries provided by the client on diskette or in another electronic form, and electronic versions of general and technical dictionaries.

A terminology management system must, of course, help the translator use technical terms consistently. There are several kinds of consistency required: consistency within a document, consistency across multiple documents from the same client, and consistency with standardized terminology. When a single translator produces an entire document in one sitting, document-internal consistency can be achieved simply through short-term memory. But when a large document is split up into segments to be translated in parallel by several translators, tools for achieving consistency become much more important. Such tools are also needed when an additional document from a certain client must use terminology consistently with the previous document, which may have been translated months or years ago. In a paper-based approach, consistency is achieved by having one card file which every translator must consult, and individual translators who make notes on new terms or variations on old terms give these notes to a coordinator who updates the card file. In an electronic approach, there must also be the possibility of accessing shared information and contributing personal notes to the database coordinator.

The sharing of terminology applies not just to in-house translators. In a paper-based approach to terminology, it is expensive for a client to share terminology with free-lance translators to ensure consistency. Terminology files must be printed out on paper and distributed. If, as is often the case, the terminology file is extensive and rapidly changing, this sharing becomes a significant expense (and a bottleneck if the document to be translated is sent electronically while the terminology book must be mailed because of its size). With electronic terminology management making distance sharing of rapidly changing information more feasible, there will probably be rising expectations on the part of clients who are aware of new possibilities. If a free-lance has a direct relationship with a client, the client might want to transmit to the freelance the source text along with an electronic version of any terminological data that should be used during the translation. This implies the need for either a universal terminology management package (which is unlikely) or a universal terminology interchange format. If a freelance works through a service bureau, that service bureau has a responsibility (seldom recognized at present) to obtain terminology files from the client or to build them up for the client and to provide them to each translator who does work for the client.

The increasing emphasis on sharing and the gradual recognition by clients that consistency does not happen magically but rather must be ensured through shared access to terminology, raises the issue of providing to the client, along with a target language text, an update to the client's terminology database. This is a valuable service, and its cost should be negotiated up-front, not after the translation job is completed.

The third criterion (besides flexibility and support for consistency) to keep in mind when selecting a terminology management package is efficiency. One aspect of efficiency is rapid access to the information stored in a terminology file. You do not want to look through a card file from front to back to find the relevant card. In an electronic terminology database, you want to be able to search a database sequentially if needed, but the normal way to access it is by typing in a term (or part of a term) and asking the system to consult an index allowing instant access to an entry. When you either do not know or do not remember the appropriate target language term for a particular domain and client, electronic lookup can be much faster than consulting a card file. Although the primary access to a translation-oriented terminology file is usually the source language term, a terminology management package should also provide a way to set up additional indexes to the data, such as an index by target language term or by abbreviation.

Another aspect of efficiency is not having to type unnecessary information. Once the desired target language term is found, it should be possible to paste it into the target text without retyping it. This is not only a question of efficiency but of consistency, since hand typing of a long term can easily introduce minor inconsistencies in spelling, capitalization, and punctuation.

Often, such as when a term is used many times in the same document, there will be no need to access the terminology file in the same way that it is accessed when the target language term is unknown. It may be well-known, and the translator may be tired of typing it. For such cases, the terminology management package should provide a mechanism for the translator to devise short personal acronyms (usually two or three letters) for longer terms and associate these short forms with the full forms. Then, when it is time to insert one of these well-known terms into the target text, the translator need only type the short form with some indication that it is a short form, leaving the automatic lookup and expansion to the software.

Presently almost every translator uses a word processor. It is likely that in the near future, most translators will expand their level-one tools to include word processing utilities (and desktop publishing if needed), telecommunications software, and terminology software. The most crucial unresolved issue is the universal acceptance of an electronic terminology interchange format. However, the Terminology and the Translation and Computers Committees of the American Translators Association are participating in an international effort to define and standardize such a format.

These level-one tools can all be used when the source text is handed to the translator on paper or transmitted by fax. Terminology management can even be used when terminological data come to the translator on paper. In such a case, source and target terms plus appropriate descriptive and administrative information can be entered into the translator's terminology database when a term first appears in the source text. However, most source texts are now available as word processing files, and many terminology files are available in electronic form. This suggests new possibilities, which we will call level two.

4.2 LEVEL TWO

Level two includes all the features of level one, but adds additional features that require the source text and associated terminology files to be available in machine readable form. The most interesting level-two features are text analysis, automatic dictionary lookup, and bilingual text retrieval. Since most documents are not currently supplied in machine readable form, these features are not yet commonly used. Unfortunately, it is not usually cost-effective to scan a paper document and put it into machine-readable form using OCR software, since it takes too much time to correct the errors made by the OCR software. Hence this section is somewhat futuristic, since it assumes that both the source text and any client-specific terminology entries are available in electronic form. Let us hope that this future is not too distant.

Text Analysis

The first step in any level-two processing is text analysis, that is, automatic analysis of the source text. This consists of dividing the source text into segments, such as titles, paragraphs, sentences and words. In most cases, the basic structure of the target text is required to be the same as that of the source text. Yet typically the translator must enter the format codes to set up the structure of the target text from scratch. At level two, software should allow the translator to generate a "skeleton" target text based on the source text. This "skeleton" target text would duplicate the source text's structure but put the words of the source text in some kind of non-printing comment. They could be used for reference purposes during translation but be set off to be automatically deleted if desired when the translation is completed. Another possibility for text analysis, which applies mainly to very large source texts, is indexing to permit a rapid search of all occurrences of particular combinations of words, even if they are not contiguous. This can be useful in preparing terminology files.

Automatic Dictionary Lookup

Another component of level two is automatic dictionary lookup. This can take several forms. A spell check can be useful in identifying some terms, the main problem being the identification of terms which consist entirely of words which are found in the spell check word list. There is even some research being done into the automatic identification of terms, combining text analysis and dictionary lookup, although at present the accuracy level of such software is not high. An alternative approach to automatic terminology identification is to select a segment of text, either automatically or manually (using a mouse or some other mechanism), and ask the automatic dictionary lookup to produce a list of single and multi-word terms that are found in the segment. The terms that are found in the segment of source text should be marked and linked to the appropriate term entry. This process can improve consistency by reminding the translator that certain terms have a standard translation equivalent. The translator can then put together the sentences of the target text, pulling in standard target language terms without having to type the source language term. Sometimes an argument is given for machine translation on the basis that nearly unreadable machine translation is worthwhile just because the technical terms are used more consistently than in human translation because humans are unwilling to use terms consistently. Hopefully, this argument will evaporate as translators begin using level-two lookup and focus on consistency in terminology. Then machine translation, sometimes with human postediting, will be used on other grounds than terminological consistency.

Bilingual Text Retrieval

As paired source and target texts are stored over an extended period of time, a new possibility unfolds: bilingual text retrieval. Suppose that all source and target texts worked on by a translator or, even better, a group of translators, are stored in a data base where segments of source and target text are linked and every word is indexed. This alignment and indexing process produces what is often called bitext (a term coined by Brian Harris of the University of Ottawa). Then, when a difficult term or phrase appears and no immediate solution is found in the translator's terminology database, the bilingual database can be consulted. Occurrences of the source term or phrase can be displayed, along with the segment of target text which is associated with the source segment and which therefore most likely contains the translation equivalent of the source term or phrase. Clients with large document databases could supply them on CD-ROM to translators or could make the database available by modem. Bilingual text synchronization also suggests the possibility of after-the-fact checking translations to make sure that standard equivalents of client-crucial terms have been used consistently, with exceptions flagged for a human reviewer to analyze.

For the case of the translation of a minor revision of a previously translated text, there are tools which implement what is often called "translation memory." Translation memory retrieves from a bitext database the translation of segments that are unchanged or nearly unchanged, resulting in potentially large gains in efficiency.

SGML (Standard Generalized Markup Language)

All documents have some format, although this may be somewhat implicit. The way the format of a text is represented in the text, that is, the way the text is "marked up," is very important to all level-two processing. There are two kinds of markup, presentational and descriptive. Presentational markup specifies such information as the size of the margins, the font name, the point size, centering, and other aspects of how the text is to be presented on the printed page. All text must ultimately receive presentational markup before it can be printed out. But text is more useable, especially in computer processing, if its basic representation is in descriptive markup. Descriptive markup defines units of text, such as a title, a main heading, a secondary heading, a paragraph, or a sentence by their function, not their presentation on the printed page. Then, a table of correspondence between descriptive markup and presentational markup allows a software program to make a presentational version of the document for printing. The most widely used system of descriptive markup is called SGML (Standard Generalized Markup Language).

A text which has been marked up in SGML can be analyzed much more accurately than a text with only presentational markup available, since units such as paragraphs are marked explicitly rather than implicitly. In particular, a "skeleton" document in SGML would be much easier to work with than one with presentational markup. Some clients are beginning to ask for target texts with SGML markup. This is now feasible since at least one major word processing vendor, WordPerfect, has announced their intention to sell a software package that converts between WordPerfect files and SGML files. The only caveat is that for the conversion to work smoothly, the WordPerfect file must use "styles" (a feature of standard WordPerfect) to mark the format. For example, an "emphasis" style might be used to turn bold on before a word or phrase and to turn it off afterward rather than explicitly choosing a different font each time.

4.3 LEVEL THREE

Level three involves the use of machine translation by a translator. The machine translation system can be installed on the translator workstation, or it can be a remote system to which you send a file of source text and receive a file of translated text. Of course, machine translation does not apply to every text. It is most applicable to texts which are restricted to a narrow well-defined domain for which there exists a machine translation system which handles the source and target languages and which has been "tuned" to that domain. Of course, the source text must be available in a machine-readable form with a compatible format.

Machine translation is further discussed in the preceding Vasconcellos essay. The point of this section is that when a translator becomes involved in using post-editing machine translation, the translator workstation is not discarded. The same hardware and software components needed for levels one and two will also be used at level three, along with extra software specific to level three.

5. Conclusion

Nearly every translator has at least a minimal translator workstation which functions at level one. In the next few years, most translators will acquire additional level-one components, and we will probably see more and more text production which involves level two and level three. Translator workstations should evolve to better support the translator in serving remote clients, maintaining high quality through consistent use of terminology, and increasing efficiency through integration with the rest of the document production path and better retrieval of documents, terminology, and text segments during the translation process.

Obviously, the story of the translator workstation is just beginning. It promises to be an exciting one.

Section 5:

Current Economic and Legal Issues

Translation and Interpreting in the 90s: Major Economic and Legal Issues Confronting the Community

BERNARD BIERMAN

If there is any one thing that has characterized translation and interpreting (both as professions and industries) in the United States in the first eight decades of the twentieth century, it has been the good fortune of having existed and operated, and perhaps even thrived in "safe harbor" environment, i.e., free of certain problems of an economic and legal nature, particularly taxation-connected, that have beset numerous other professions and industries. Indeed, a perusal of the vast literature generated by the translation and interpreting professions in the past 30–40 years clearly evidences the absence of concern over such questions as tax status and legal status, the latter particularly in respect of the courts and numerous government agencies, Federal, State and local. However, the 1990s have seen some radical changes come about in the wake of new tax regulations, new court decisions and perhaps more significantly, changes in the socio-linguistic fiber of this nation that have thrust both translators and interpreters into a position of being more essential. This article will discuss some of those changes and attendant concerns for language professionals.

I. The Independent Contractor Question

It is widely accepted among professional translators and interpreters that one of the more attractive features—if not the most attractive feature—in the field is independence. Indeed, the commercial or business sector of translation and interpreting is composed of small or independent businesspersons, organized either as small businesses (referred to as "translation service companies," or "translation agencies" or "translation bureaus") or as individual contractors (also referred to as "freelance" or "independent" translators/interpreters). Notwithstanding the recent entry into the industry of such corporate giants as AT&T and Rank-Xerox, translation and interpreting as a commercial endeavor still remains, in relative terms, in the category of "small business." For as long as anyone in the field can remember and for as long as written records have been kept, translators and interpreters (whether classified as companies or independent individuals) have been free to engage in their professions without having to concern themselves with compendia of government rules and regulations, and worse, monitoring.

This has been markedly true in respect of one characteristic peculiar to the industry, namely the contractual relationship that exists between the translation service company and the freelance translator or interpreter. Within the specific area of taxes and tax status, that relationship has always enjoyed little or no questioning by government tax authorities. Clearly, until the end of the 1980s, each party in that relationship maintained sole responsibility for the payment of taxes (specifically Federal taxes and social security contributions). For example, the payment of a fee by a translation company to a freelance sub-contractor was viewed and treated as compensation paid for services rendered within a domain of pristine independence. The Internal Revenue Service, the chief tax collection agency of the United States Government, looked to each party individually for the payment of the appropriate taxes, and clearly those parties remained individually liable for such payment. However, the Tax Reform Act of 1986 changed that, albeit indirectly. The indirect change came about as a result of Congress being unwilling to legislate the type of tax treatment on independent contractor relationships and compensation which the Internal Revenue Service had lobbied for, namely to provide an across-the-board 20% withholding-at-source on compensation paid to independent contractors. (The Congress, however, did enact legislation providing for such withholding-at-source on other types of compensation). It must be interjected at this point that the IRS' request for withholding-at-source legislation on independent contractor compensation was based in part on abuses that appeared to be growing and/or erroneous classification of employees as independent contractors. Unfortunately, legitimate independent contractor relationships—such as those existing in the translation and interpreting community—also became the subject of intense focus by the IRS. Given operating and budgetary considerations, the full thrust of the IRS's focus on independent contractor relationships was not felt until around 1990, and the initial reports by translation companies selected for the Revenue Service's new procedure, called the "Employment Tax Compliance Check," started to filter in around 1991. These reports indicated that the IRS was questioning certain practices followed by and between translation companies and independent translators that had for decades been considered perfectly legitimate and consonant with tax regulations.

The IRS's new approach for determining whether an independent contractor was truly an independent contractor and not an employee is based upon three basic elements:

1. The common law.
2. The facts and circumstances test.
3. The (IRS's) 20 factors (or questions).

The common law test used by the IRS is based upon the old British common law precept of the **master-servant** relationship. Translating that into modern application, it means determining whether the party requesting the services (in this case, the translation company) controls or can exercise control over the party rendering the services (in this case, the independent translator) in respect of **how** the services are to be rendered, **where** the services are to be rendered, and **when** the services are to be rendered. Taken at face value, the "how," "where" and "when" elements could easily render any independent contractor relationship null and void, for the "how" could be a simple directive from a translation company to a freelance translator to provide the translation on a 3.5" diskette in MicroSoft Word, and thus be interpreted as the translation company exercising **control** as in a master-servant relationship, or in more modern terms, in an employer-employee relationship. It is at the point that the "facts and circumstances" test comes into play, and even the most zealous IRS auditor would acknowledge that such a request is nothing more than a **commercial order,** devoid of all trappings of control. Likewise would be the "when" element ("translation required by next Monday"). The "where" factor, although usually not even a factor in the traditional translation company-freelance translator relationship, could and does become a component when the IRS's 20 factors are brought into play. And it is the application of some of these factors, taken with or without the common law and facts and circumstances tests that can bring and have brought problems to many in the translation and interpreting field.

About half of the IRS's 20 factors have applicability to the traditional translation agency-independent translator relationship. Only two of these will be discussed in this article, and this, with relative brevity:

A. Rendering of On-Premises Services:

An independent translator rendering services on the premises of a translation company, even at irregular intervals, runs the risk of being classified an employee for that period of time when the services are rendered on-premises. Such a reclassification would mean that income taxes and social security contributions would be withheld from the translator's compensation. But those taxes would be withheld in accordance with employee withholding tables; these tables do not take into consideration **business** expenses. And the business expenses of an independent practitioner reclassified to "employee" would not disappear: the end-result would be a *de jure* employee but a *de facto* business person whose taxes would be withheld at source on **gross** compensation and not on **net** compensation. The consequent cash-flow problems could be considerable. For the translation company, the impact of having to re-classify an independent contractor to an employee could be more severe. The translation company would have to match the translator's social security contributions, and make the appropriate contributions to the Federal Unemployment Fund. To exacerbate this situation, since the Federal government regularly reports such changes in classification to State and local governments, the translation company would then find itself facing additional contributions to State Unemployment Funds, State Disability Funds and Workers' Compensation Funds. Given that reclassifications are made during audits, there is also the matter of penalties and interest that would have to be considered. Finally, a reclassification of an independent translator to employee would necessitate for the translation company an increase in administrative chores, including but certainly not limited to the filing of a myriad of payroll tax returns and attendant reports.

Although freelance translators working occasionally or at irregular intervals on the premises of a translation company is not the norm, nonetheless there are sufficient instances of this practice to warrant concern. The problem appears with those companies holding government translation contracts stipulating that no documents may be removed from the company's office. This stipulation necessitates having, even on an *ad hoc* basis, bona fide independent translators render their services on-premises. The IRS now takes a very dim view of that practice—even if it is occasional. To wit:

> If the work performed on the premises of the person or company for whom the services are performed, that factor suggests control over the person performing the services, especially if the work could be done elsewhere.

The "safety valve" here is the phrase "especially if the work could be done elsewhere." If the IRS recognizes a stricture on the removal of documents from the company's office, then it would appear that the IRS would refrain from reclassifying the translator as an employee. However, linked to this rendering of on-premises services is the IRS's equally dim view of a company providing equipment and/or materials to an independent contractor. One can thus see that these 20 factors are not exactly autonomous; rather a so-called "violation" of one could easily mean—because of the linkage—a "violation" of three or four.

B) Rendering of Services by a Freelance Translator to One or Two Translation Companies:

It is fairly well-established, even in the absence of statistical data, that a good portion of the freelance translator market is a "part-time" market, i.e., translators holding regular employment but rendering their services after-hours and/or on weekends. These part-time freelance translators usually tend to have one or two clients, since time obviously precludes having more. Let us read what the IRS says about this subject:

> If a person performs more than de minimis services for a multiple of unrelated persons or companies AT THE SAME TIME, that factor generally indicates that the worker is an independent contractor.

Accordingly, a freelance translator, whether full-time or part-time, who has just one client or perhaps two clients, could be easily viewed by the IRS as an employee of those "clients," more especially if the bulk of the translator's income is derived from one of the two. Again, as in the foregoing example, there is a linkage that operates here. The following may be called factors "c" and "d": (c) Does the freelance translator have a continuing relationship with the translation company? (d) Does the freelance translator make his or her services available to the general public?

For the former factor, the IRS says:

> A continuing relationship between the person rendering the service and the person or company for whom the service is performed indicates that an employee-employer relationship exists. A continuing relationship may exist where work is performed at frequently recurring although irregular intervals.

For the latter factor, the IRS says:

> The fact that a person makes his or her services available to the general public on a REGULAR or CONSISTENT basis indicates an independent contractor relationship.

The IRS spells out five sub-factors here, two of which would have direct applicability to the translation and interpreting field:

- That the independent translator list his or her name and services in a business directory.
- That the independent translator advertise his or her services.

All of the foregoing has focused on the relationship between the translation company and the freelance translator. Nothing has been said about the freelance *interpreter,* and for good reason.

There is reason to believe that in an Employment Tax Compliance Check, the services rendered by a freelance interpreter under contract to a translation agency would be treated somewhat differently from the services rendered by a freelance translator under contract to a translation agency. The language of the IRS (especially if the common law precepts and the facts and circumstances test are taken into account) is quite ominous, to wit:

> This relief [from payment of employment taxes] is not available, however, to a business that furnishes technical service specialists (including but not limited to engineers, computer programmers and systems analysts) to clients. In these cases, the employment relationship between the business and the specialist will be determined in the common law rules.

If we accept that in an independent interpreter-translation agency relationship, the latter oftentimes exercises far more control than in the translator-agency relationship (e.g., specifying the place of services, mode of dress, criteria of behavior, etc.), the independent interpreter could very well end up being classified as an employee. In fact, this author has knowledge of a few isolated cases not involving the IRS but State Labor Departments which are alleging this very thing: that the translation company is acting as an **agency** (as in **employment agency**) when it assigns interpreters to a specific job, and is exercising controls that fall within the common law's master-servant precept.

When the independent contractor question initially arose, the reaction in the translation and interpreting community ranged from ambivalence to cock-sureness, i.e., that the translation company-freelance translator (and interpreter) relationship was so totally independent that no tax authority could even question it. While there is still a great deal of ambivalence in the community, the cock-sureness appears to have dissipated, and for good reason too: a tax investigation is very expensive, and that does not say anything about the stress suffered by the taxpayer during an audit and while waiting for the final determination.

It is the author's belief that to label the independent contractor question "a translation agency problem" would be erroneous and certainly short-sighted, as much as it would be to label the home-office deduction question *(vide infra)* a "freelance" problem. If in this last decade of this century translation and interpreting have been unable to attain the goal of public recognition as professions, they have attained a far more dubious goal: tax visibility. And that is indeed a concern for the entire community.

II. The Home Office Tax Deduction

In mid-January of 1993, the United States Supreme Court issued a ruling in a tax case that could have wide-ranging repercussions on both independent translators and interpreters. Here again, the genesis lies in the Tax Reform Act of 1986, in which Congress attempted to place greater restrictions on the tax deductibility of an office in the home. As in numerous cases of tax legislation, the intent of Congress is often subject to interpretation both by the Executive Branch (and the Internal Revenue Service) and the Judicial Branch. The term "**principal place of business**" formed the crux of this particular tax case, for the Revenue Service viewed the term in a much more restrictive light than did the particular taxpayer (and ostensibly his accountant and/or tax attorney). At the lower levels, the courts ruled for the taxpayer, but at the all-critical Supreme Court level, the IRS prevailed.

The case which resulted in this landmark decision involved an anesthesiologist who took a tax deduction for one room in his home which he used for maintaining patient records, speaking with patients over the telephone and conducting other business related to his profession. The hospitals at which he rendered his services did not provide him with office space for him to carry out those essential duties.

The IRS argued that the physician was not entitled to deduct the use of that room in his home because it was not his "**principal place of business.**" The IRS contended that the hospitals where the physician rendered his services constituted the "principal place of business." By an 8 to 1 margin, the Supreme Court ruled in favor of the IRS and did so by establishing (a) a very narrow definition of "principal place of business" in which the key components are **time and order of essentiality of the services**, and (b) by applying that definition and the components thereof only to those whose business is conducted from or within a residence. To put this into relief, and at the same time to indicate the impact that this decision can have on the translation and interpreting communities—and particularly the latter—what follows is a paraphrase of one of the key passages in the high court's ruling; however, it should be carefully noted that this paraphrase extends only to the replacement of the words "**treatment**" and "**hospital**" with the words "**interpreting**" and "**courtroom**" (or "**conference room**"), respectively:

> The actual interpreting was the essence of the professional service. We can assume that careful planning and study were required in advance of performing the interpreting, and all acknowledge that this was done in the home office. But the actual interpreting was the most significant event in the professional transaction. The home office activities, from an objective standpoint, must be regarded as less important to the business of the taxpayer than the tasks he performed at the courtroom (or conference room).
>
> A comparison of the time spent by the taxpayer further supports a determination that the home office was not the principal place of business. The 10 or 15 hours per week spent in the home office measured against the 30 to 35 hours per week spent at the courtroom and/or conference room are insufficient to render the home office the principal place of business in light of all of the cir-

cumstances of the case. That the office may have been essential is not controlling.

It must be re-emphasized that the Court's decision in respect of "principal place of business" applies solely to the case where a business is conducted from a residence. It would not apply and does not apply to a case in which, for example, an interpreter rents space in an **office building**, is present in that office for a mere 5-10 hours a week, and renders his service at the courtroom or in the conference room for some 30-35 hours a week. In this latter instance, the expenses for the premises in the office building are **fully deductible**! In other words, there is one test for the goose and another for the gander.

The effect of this decision on a major segment of the translation and interpreting community cannot be minimized. In some which way every independent translator and every independent interpreter (save for those who rent commercial space for the conduct of their business) will be affected. Following are some synoptic examples of how this ruling will affect [independent] translators and interpreters:

A. Part-Time Freelance Translators

A translator works 40 hours a week at his or her regular job (which is also that of a translator) earning a yearly salary of $35,000. The translator also renders independent translation services from an office in the home, spending an average of 20 hours a week there, and earning $15,000 a year from those services. Using the test of **relative essentiality** and **time spent at each location**, the "principal place of business" would be easily determined as the translator's regular job. A deduction for the home office would be disallowed.

B. Full- and Part-Time Freelance Interpreters

Here it is not even a case of holding regular employment. Whereas the translator—with some exceptions—renders the services from a specific and usually-permanent place, not so with the interpreter. Except for some very rare occasion such as an overseas telephone conference, the interpreter's principal place of business (as now defined by the Supreme Court) is the courtroom, or conference room, or jail cell or hospital bed, or the tour bus or cruise ship. These are [some of] the places where interpreters render their services. Applying the Court's reasoning in the case of the anesthesiologist to interpreters, it can be said that **the essence of the professional service provided by the interpreter is to provide communication between persons speaking different languages, not maintaining client records.**

C. FULL-TIME FREELANCE TRANSLATORS

Here deductibility for an office in the home is not in question, for a freelance translator whose office is in the home and who derives virtually all income from such freelance translation services meets all of the Supreme Court's "principal place of business" tests. The problem here is so-called "audit visibility." A deduction for an office in the home is automatically suspect, and now even more so with the Supreme Court's decision. Indeed, as soon as the Supreme Court ruling was issued, the IRS immediately suspended distribution of its Publication 587 (Home Office Deductions) to include the Court's definition in a revised edition. To determine precisely who is using an office in the home and taking a deduction therefor, the IRS has devised a new form—Form 8829—which is appended to Schedule C, the form most commonly used by freelance translators and interpreters. Form 8829 is used exclusively for listing and detailing those expenses connected with the home office. Both the old and new Schedule C make no such provision. A filing of a Form 8829 is bound to receive IRS scrutiny, if not an appointment for an audit. And here as in the independent contractor issue, an adverse determination on an IRS audit is immediately reported to State tax authorities. Finally, it must not be forgotten that the burden of proof in any tax-related matter rests with the taxpayer. The words of Justice Harry Blackmun ring like the bells of Notre Dame: "A deduction from gross income is a matter of grace, not right."

III. The Certified Translation Question

The terms "certified translation," "official translation," "certified translator," "accredited translator," "official translator," "certified interpreter," "court-certified interpreter" and "Federally-certified interpreter," along with some variations on, the foregoing, are all not necessarily new. However, what is new is the confusion that has arisen, particularly in the past five or so years, over the precise definitions of those terms, and this, both within practical and legal frameworks. Moreover, the confusion is not merely limited to lay persons, attorneys, judges and administrators, but extends to translators and interpreters themselves.

The genesis of this confusion is quite complex, and therefore little attempt will be made in this section to address or analyze those complexities; rather, the attempt will be to focus on certain of these terms and their definitions, along with some appropriate background.

A. CERTIFIED TRANSLATION: DEFINITION

By legal definition, application, usage and tradition, a certified translation is one in which the translator or translation service company affirms or swears under oath that the translation is a true, accurate and correct rendering in one language from another, often accompanied by the proviso "to his/her/its best knowledge and ability." This affirmation or sworn statement is embodied in what is called a **Certificate of Accuracy**. The Certificate of Accuracy is signed by the translator or authorized representative/officer of the translation company before a Notary or Commissioner of Deeds.

When a Certificate of Accuracy is appended to a translation, the document is generally or commonly referred to as a **"certified translation."** It is sometimes also referred to as an **"official translation."** Certified translations are commonly used for court purposes (e.g., translation of documents to be used as evidence in legal actions, whether civil or criminal) or for administrative purposes (e.g., translation of birth and similar certificates for submission of a government agency). Certified translations are not necessarily limited to legal or administrative proceedings; a requirement of a certified translation could be a mere security formality as in the case of presentation of translations to the Food and Drug Administration in support of a new drug application.

Finally, it should be borne in mind that a certified translation is not necessarily one of a "legal" document, a kind of catch-all or convenient term used both by lay people and translators to describe a document couched in the parlance and even jargon of law or legal administration. Any translated document embodying any subject matter may require certification. As alluded to above, a translation of a report on a particular medication, replete with complex chemical and biochemical terms, may require certification before it can be submitted to the appropriate government agency or to a court that may be hearing a patent infringement case.

B. Background of the Translation "Problem"

While the submission of certified translations to courts and other administrative entities is certainly nothing novel, in more recent times there has been a marked increase in volume, ascribable among others to the "internationalization" of this country and to the ever-growing number of immigrants and other persons (not fluent in or conversant with English) requiring the services of the courts and/or other administrative entities. Indeed, these trends constitute a principal reason for the remarkable growth of the U.S. translation and interpreting industry in the past two or so decades.

It is well known, however, and more or less acknowledged in the translation community that this increase in the volume of translated documentation has brought some significant problems, particularly the submission of translations by persons or entities purportedly lacking essential skills, the product thereof being inaccurate and/or incomprehensible translations. Unfortunately (or fortunately, depending on one's legal philosophy), there are few alternatives available to ensure that only those qualified to translate will have free run of the field. "Bad" translations are part of our scenery, just as "bad" writing is part of it.

C. The Legal Fiber of Translation

In many nations throughout the world, certain legal strictures are placed upon translators and the translation profession. State certification is one such vehicle and State licensing is another. Certain nations which use certification or licensing apply it only to a specified group of translators, e.g., "legal" or "court" translators, while others are "free to roam the countryside." In our country, translation is viewed (for purposes of law) as one branch of the communications arts, and therefore falls under the full protection of the First Amendment to the Constitution. Indeed, such proposals as the licensing of writers (Nevada, 1963), journalists (Puerto Rico, ca. 1980) and public relations specialists (Massachusetts, 1992) died quick deaths even before they could reach a legislative committee hearing. Clearly, as *The New York Times* put it in an editorial, "Licensing [of journalists] doesn't have a prayer of surviving a test in the United States Supreme Court, which will view the licensing of anyone who makes a living through the use, application and implementation of language as the original British sin that gave birth to the Constitution's First Amendment." Therefore, translation has remained, and will doubtless remain a so-called "free" or "uncontrolled" profession.

D. Traditional Handling of Certified Translations

In view of the foregoing and other closely-related reasons, courts, government agencies and other users of certified translations have limited themselves to setting forth the following requirements for acceptance of a certified translation:

1. That the translation be accurate, readable, communicative and comprehensible to all parties concerned.
2. That the translation be done by a person or entity who/which can evidence the fact that he/she/it is engaged in the profession or business of providing translation services. In most instances the exhibiting of a business letterhead or the submission of a photocopy of a commercial advertisement placed in a trade or commercial directory will satisfy the requirement that the translator or translation company is engaged in the translation services business or profession. (Most, if not all recipients or users of certified translations require that the Certificate of Accuracy be on the letterhead of the translator or translation company.) Some users or recipients of certified translations require an additional statement (usually embodied in the Certificate of Accuracy) that summarizes the translator's or translation company's credentials.
3. That the translation *not* be done by a person or entity who/which has a vested interest in the subject matter of the document being translated, or who/which may be a party to the transaction embodied in the document being translated. In other words, a [professional] translator is precluded from submitting a certified translation of his or her own foreign language divorce decree. This prohibition even extends to an attorney whose own office has prepared a translation for that attorney's client.

E. Reference Lists of Translator/Translation Companies

There are numerous courts and administrative entities (hereinafter referred to as the "government") which maintain so-called reference lists of translators/translation companies. These lists are usually formulated on the basis of the government's past favorable experience with a particular translator or translation company. However, a few restrictions operate here:

1. The government cannot recommend any one particular translator/translation company to an inquiring party. Rather, the inquiring party must be informed that he/she/it is free to select whichever individual or company is most suitable for the task at hand. And the inquiring party must be further informed that he/she/it is free to select or use a translator/translation company who/which is not on the list, albeit with the understanding that the **correctness and accuracy of the translation is the ultimate test for acceptance.**
2. The government may not restrict such list in number. Any translator/translation company meeting the tests outlined in section d) above must be included in that list. However, the government is free to omit from such list a translator or translation company who/which in advertising other commercial representations uses such inclusion in this reference list to deceive or defraud the public by such statements as "Certified by the _____ Court," or "Accredited by the _____ Agency." The government does not certify or accredit translators and/or translation companies.

F. "Accredited" Translator—"Certified Translator"

If we call the product a "certified translation," why should we not call its producer a "certified translator?" And therein lies some of the confusion. A certified translator does not exist in law in this country. There are no State-sponsored or supported examinations, the passing of which would entitle a translator to call himself or herself a "certified translator." Likewise for the term "accredited." Both of these terms have unfortunately been bandied about by many translators, some of whom believe that acceptance by the government of a translation under certified conditions automatically makes them "certified" translators. The use of "accredited" translator appears to be linked to an examination given by the American Translators Association (ATA).

The examination of the American Translators Association consists of translating three passages totalling together approximately 800–900 words. The examinations are given for various language combinations, e.g., French-to-English, Japanese-to-English, English-to-Spanish. In order to take the exam, the candidate must be a member of the Association. There are no other pre-qualifying conditions for group sittings. (A new policy has been instituted, however, requiring passage of the practice test in order to be eligible for an individual sitting.) If the candidate passes the examination, an accreditation certificate is issued for the specific language combination elected by the candidate. The title given to the successful candidate is "ATA-accredited translator, (language combination)." There is no limit on the number of language combination exams a candidate may take. The Association insists that its members use the proper nomenclature, including an indication of the language combination following the term "ATA-accredited translator." The accreditation and the accreditation certificate or certificates lapse upon termination of membership in the Association for any reason whatsoever. In its literature, the Association describes the accreditation exam as a "test for determining whether a candidate possesses the basic skills of a translator." Approximately 1300 current members of the American Translators Association have the title of "ATA-Accredited."

However, ATA accreditation is not officially recognized by any government entity.

G. Translators and Interpreters

There is a distinct difference between a translator and interpreter, notwithstanding the fact that within the language community they are called "sister professions."

The differences between the two reside in the fact that the processing of written language occurs in a different part of the brain from where the processing of oral language takes place. Development is another factor, as witnessed by the common occurrence of a child or teenager being able to interpret effectively for parents unable to speak the local or national language. Yet when the same child is asked to translate even a simple piece of writing, a paralysis immediately occurs.

It is well-known in the language community that there are numerous interpreters who are incapable of performing written translation, and it is just as well known that there are numerous translators capable of translating from eight languages who are unable to speak any one of them with fluency or fluidity. There are numerous articles about this phenomenon in the language community's literature and in the literature of that emerging field called cognitive science.

A prospective user of translation and/or interpreting services would do well to bear this carefully in mind. (Unfortunately, several agencies of the U.S. government, e.g., the Drug Enforcement Administration (DEA) and

Federal Bureau of Investigation (FBI), appear to be ignorant of this phenomenon and the distinctions deriving from it. The DEA has a directive that in respect of certain languages calls for the translation to be done or at a minimum verified by a **Federally-certified court INTERPRETER!**)

H. FEDERALLY-CERTIFIED COURT INTERPRETER

It is an unquestionable fact that our courts are more and more having to face a language problem. This fact was recognized by the enactment of the Court Interpreters Act. In essence, the purpose of this law was to provide the U.S. courts with a corps of skilled professional interpreters, with such skills being determined by an examination.

The reputation of that examination appears to be quite good, and those who pass it certainly seem worthy of the title "Federally-certified Court Interpreter." As of the time of writing this article, the examinations are limited to Spanish, Haitian-Creole and certain Navajo languages.

However, there are two important points that should be remembered about the Court Interpreters Act.

1. That the government maintains the option, if not the right—where practical and whenever applicable—to use or employ or sub-contract to (before all others) an interpreter holding Federal certification. The key words here are **use, employ** and **sub-contract**. The government more and more appears to be following this practice in the following two particular instances: (i) where it is the plaintiff and (ii) where the defendant waives the right to use his/her/its own interpreter, or requests that the government provide an interpreter.
2. One does not have to hold Federal certification in order to be able to interpret in the courts or before some administrative entity. Indeed, a defendant maintains the right to use his/her/its own interpreter, who does not have to be Federally-certified.

(Additional particulars regarding the *modus operandi* of the Court Interpreters Act may be found in the United States Code, Section 1827.)

Finally, the Act makes no mention whatsoever that certification of an interpreter includes qualification to prepare written translations.

California, New Mexico and Utah have also instituted a procedure for measuring the qualifications of interpreters assigned or under contract to the various State courts. New Jersey is in the process of instituting one, and it can be safely projected that by the turn of the century there will be at least a dozen states, if not more, that will have adopted measures to determine the qualifications of court and administrative interpreters.

Conclusions

There has been a marked trend in the translation and interpreting communities to shy away from what could be called the daily exigencies of life, and rather focus on things intellectual or even ethereal. Perhaps this is ascribable to the "psyche" of the translator and interpreter, i.e., introverted, "bookish," esoteric. However, the three issues discussed here might even awaken the most inward looking translator or interpreter, for two of them, and perhaps even the third, have a discernible economic complexion, and all of us—irrespective of particular interests—must eat. Looking at this from a somewhat more positive angle, all three issues present what I would call refreshing challenges to the translation and interpreting communities. In respect of the independent contractor and home office deduction issues, the challenge is to make known to those in positions of authority that translation and interpreting have features peculiar to them and those features cannot be lumped with or compared to those of other professions or occupations. An interpreter in a courtroom is not a physician in an operating room. The challenge is to reassert to and reinforce for persons in positions of influence and authority that the relationships that are particular to the business of translation and interpreting ring of pristine independence, that to say or infer otherwise is a grotesque twisting of the term independence. And in respect of the third issue, the challenge facing the community is to undertake a broad educational program, a program that will not only educate users and prospective users of translation and interpreting services, but will also educate those already in the business and the profession and those who will become its future practitioners.

Section 6:

Translator/Interpreter Training in the U.S.

The Role of the University in the Professionalization of the Translator

ANNE CORDERO

The role of the university in the professionalization of the translator is still controversial, especially in the United States, although university translation studies programs have multiplied during the last decade.[1] In addition to the programs already in place there are others in the planning stage at this moment. The present trend towards professionalization, characterized in the U.S. by new university-based programs whose students are granted diplomas after successfully completing the course of study, is parallelled in European countries by a shift away from vocational language schools and technical colleges to the university.

If university-based translator education programs are still controversial, it is because the **necessity** and **effectiveness** of such programs in the professionalization of translators and their legitimacy as a university discipline are being contested. I shall therefore focus on these two issues which are intimately related to the question of what constitutes a profession. In addition, while arguing my ideas on professionalization I shall suggest, though indirectly, ways of how university translator education programs may be implemented. I shall furthermore point to the university as a resource center for the translating community. Finally I shall address what, in my view, still needs to be done about the university's role in the professionalization of the translator.

One of the reasons why the role of the university in translator training and especially in the professionalization of the translator is controversial is the fact that there are a great number of translators, among them highly qualified ones, who have had no specialized training as translators at an institution of higher learning. It holds true for translators in any discipline, literary, legal or scientific-technical. They are usually experts in other fields with additional language facilities who use this expertise in their translating activity. This observation, therefore, points to one of the various charges of a university training program which is to impart to future translators those abilities and strategies which autodidacts had to acquire on their own—perhaps over a long period of time—and do this in a **systematic, methodical** way.

A further argument made when contesting the role of the university in translator education is that the greatest demand is for translators who can translate difficult technical and scientific texts for the purpose of research, technology, commerce, industry, etc. Such translators are required to have technical knowledge which they cannot acquire in the humanities. We all agree that we can only translate something we are able to understand, at least on the linguistic level. The question, therefore, posed in simplistic terms, is whether we want translators as specialists with language proficiency or linguists with scientific-technological expertise. Though phrased simplistically, the implication is obvious: we must have a clear and realistic concept of the target that a translator education program should aim for.

As the topic deals with the "professionalization" of the translator, I should specify what constitutes in my mind the actual features of a true professional status. These features, together with the requirements leading to competence in translation, define the role of the university in the professionalization of the translator.

One of the defining criteria of a "learned profession" which distinguishes it from a mere occupation or trade is a body of specialized knowledge situated on a different level from that of persons outside the discipline; it may even be inaccessible to them. This body of knowledge, although of an intellectual or theoretical nature, must be applicable in useful ways.

The linguistically related components of translator education at the university level fall into the category of this specialized body of knowledge required for translating competence. Apart from the translator's proficiency in both source and target languages, it includes, but is not limited to, the ability to analyze the source text on the levels of lexis, syntax and style. The student translator should furthermore learn to identify the intention of the author, the function of the source and the purpose of the target text; and finally he must be able to situate the text with respect to cultural information and linguistic means of the source text and the linguistic possibilities of the target text.[2] So much already has been said and written on this matter, has been analyzed and discussed from various perspectives, that hardly anything needs to be added here, except for the purpose of relating it to the subject of "professionalization."

As translating competence implies a more extended linguistic competence, such as familiarity with style, syntax, aesthetic qualities of different text types and the ability to apply this knowledge to two or more languages in such a way as to achieve adequate equivalence, it becomes clear then that competence in translating requires more than competence as acquired in foreign language classes. It is qualitatively and quantitatively different. The argument is supported by the fact that bilingual persons do not necessarily make competent translators without specialized training. It is at the same time an argument in favor of the professional status of the translator since this kind of knowledge fits the requirement of a specialized body of knowledge, one of the characteristic features of what constitutes a profession.

While a university-based translation program—and I am not just speaking of strictly literary translation studies—may place emphasis on a sound knowledge of the languages concerned, their historical development, the literature they produced, etc., it attaches equal importance to a better acquaintance with background information on the source and target cultures, with everything this implies, and a greater understanding of other disciplines which are not normally taught in foreign language departments. The extra-linguistic dimension in translator education is what distinguishes it from any other language program. It should be an integral part of any university-based translation program and consist of at least two components:

a) the teaching of general factual knowledge about the social, economic and cultural contexts of the two or more languages concerned;

b) the teaching of factual knowledge in one or several disciplines, other than the humanities, as these disciplines are taught at the university for non-major students as electives or as a minor discipline.

Acquiring extra-linguistic knowledge is a means for future translators to acquaint themselves with sufficient information as to content, specific linguistic features of the discipline, methodology and terminology. The focus should not be on the quantity of acquired knowledge, but on knowing how to find the resources, the access to needed information in a particular discipline. Developing research skills that go beyond looking up terminology is crucial for the translator. It is also an integral part of most science courses at the university level. One might even go so far as to maintain that these skills may be properly developed only in a university environment, thereby enhancing the university's role for the translator. Of course, such knowledge cannot be separated completely from knowledge of the language, for it is presented in linguistic form.

One might argue that no school can provide instruction and training in all the fields of knowledge a translator may need for special assignments. However, in a typical university environment the student is required to take core courses before he is allowed to graduate. This is one of the essential features which sets the university apart from a trade school. At George Mason University, where I teach, a student enrolled in a B.A. program needs eight hours of a laboratory science in partial fulfillment of the general education requirements. The choice a student makes from among the various sciences already indicates where his interests lie on which he may later draw in his translating activity. Similarly, the choice he makes from among the social sciences, whether economics or government, history or psychology, for example, may tell him in what direction to go as a translator. In my view, general education requirements or core courses, intended to form an educated person by exposing the student to various academic subjects, including social and natural sciences, humanities and non-western cultures, go a long way to provide a broad general background knowledge, indispensable for any translator. A minor in a certain discipline may be considered another means of acquiring extra-linguistic knowledge for future translators. As for the proper writing skills to communicate technical or scientific knowledge, the translation student at George Mason University is required to take a course taught by the English Department in Technical Writing and Editing. I do not want to imply that translator education programs should be on the undergraduate level. On the contrary, I consider the graduate level the ideal level for specialized professional curricula. However, this does not mean that *Fachwissen*, factual knowledge, cannot be acquired outside the program, either previously or simultaneously during the course of university studies. It is my opinion that university curricula accommodate well the framework for a translator education program. Therefore, when establishing such a program, a university should work with what is already in place, especially in times when budget restrictions are the order of the day. To be able to draw on the resources of other academic departments is one of the reasons why the translation program at GMU was set up as an interdisciplinary program. Edgar Faure acknowledges the university's role in translator education when he writes that "*La technique même de la traduction explique que l'Université soit appelée à jouer un rôle important dans ce domaine. Les qualités qui font de bons universitaires doivent normalement faire de bons traducteurs.*"[3] In sum, these qualities are an extensive educational background coupled with more specific knowledge in one or more disciplines, and linguistic competence in two or more languages. To this list we must add research and writing abilities.

An ideal way to obviate the reproach of an "ivory tower attitude," a reproach often heard coming from the corps of practicing translators, is to make an internship for the student translator an integral part of any university-based translation program. The purpose of an internship is to provide realistic working conditions. During the internship, which should earn the students academic credit, they will familiarize themselves with office management and equipment, client relationships and time constraints, as well as various other demands made on the working translator. In general, it is during the internship that the students discover their preferences as to the kind of translation they may want to pursue. At times an internship will lead to an offer of employment. Ideally, the internship should be done in the last semester of studies with the university instructor actively involved to follow the students' progress. A report should be required from the students at the end of the internship.

In support of the university's role in the professionalization of the translator I would like to point to a rather recent phenomenon. The traditional distinction between professional translators and philologists or linguists was considered less a difference in quality of the translation as in subject matter. The philologist was seen as limiting himself to literary and philosophical works while the professional translator earned his living with mostly technical and commercial translations. This distinction has become blurred in recent years and is no longer considered an issue as numerous academic instructors and adjunct professors supplement their income by working as professional translators and vice versa. The implication for university-based translation programs is that they can now draw on a larger pool of instructors qualified to teach other than literary translation. Besides, it is a misconception to see literary and scientific-technical translations as opposing or separate fields. A quality translation is subject to certain fundamental rules, both technical and aesthetic. Studies have shown that the defining lines between literary and scientific translations are by no means absolute, that, in fact, the teaching of the one may complement and support the other.⁴ What should define the translation instructor is the actual practice of translation, literary or other. It must be stressed, and I am aware that I do so at the risk of offending some academics, that a facility for creative writing by itself does not make a translator. Neither does expertise in literary criticism. While it is true that much of literary criticism can be applied or related to translation theory, these theoretical insights remain in a no man's land without the actual practice of translation.

The preceding remarks do not imply that translation theory should have no place in a university-based translator education program. On the contrary, in addition to the linguistic and content-related components with which critics could hardly disagree, translation theory should be an integral part of such a program. Those who oppose a theoretical approach to translation-related problems feel that theory has little relevance in practice. They also suggest that a theoretical component detracts from other educational aspects and works mostly at the expense of valuable practical training. These arguments, coming mainly from the ranks of practicing, non-university trained translators, are, in my opinion, exactly those arguments that hurt the cause of the professional status of translators the most. Because one of the defining characteristics of a learned profession is a body of specialized knowledge, translation theory constitutes an important component of this body of reference which serves as the scientific foundation, the academic underpinnings, of the discipline. It is therefore inconceivable to withhold from the students the principles that constitute their discipline. The theoretical foundation is indispensable to translators if they want to grasp the significance of their activity, approach it critically, reflect on it in order to arrive on their own at solutions. For translation theory by its very nature is linked to practice. Translating activity is concerned with decisions and choices, and the translator can make informed choices only when he/she can have recourse to the body of reference in the discipline. According to Newmark, "translation theory's main concern is to determine appropriate translation methods for the widest possible range of texts or text-categories. Further, it provides a framework of principles, restricted rules and hints for translating texts and criticizing translations, a background for problem-solving."⁵ It should be obvious that specialized knowledge requires specialized education. *Webster's* expresses this idea when it defines a profession as requiring "... often long and intensive preparation including instructional skills and methods as well as preparation in the scientific, historical or scholarly principles underlying such skills and methods...." These are all features mentioned as components of university-based translator education programs and which clearly distinguish it as intellectual knowledge, as opposed to manual dexterity or practical knowledge of a craftsman or tradesman. Most professions have established post-baccalaureate or graduate programs to prepare individuals specifically to meet these specialized educational requirements. What is more, professionals generally control the academic curricula of these programs. If it is agreed upon that a specialized body of knowledge is the most distinguishing factor of a profession and its sole purview and that normally this knowledge is acquired at an academic institution, it stands to reason that members of that profession should also determine, or have at least a hand in the curricula for the future members of that profession. The American Medical Association and the American Bar Association, for example, effectively control the educational programs in medical schools and law schools respectively; they do so directly by having some of their members serve on the faculties of these schools and indirectly by applying accreditation standards to them. Other U.S. professional organizations surely exert a similar influence on the educational processes of their future members. If the translating profession should one day succeed in shedding its image of being a trade, "*un métier,*" it needs to take the cue from other professions and do likewise.

The purpose of this article is not to argue for a programmatic accreditation of university-based translator education programs by the American Translators Association. Yet, as Peter Krawutschke points out, "The ATA could assume the role of an important link between the professional world of applied foreign languages and Academia."[6] While the ATA applies professional standards in its accrediting examinations, at present constituting practically the only means of controlling competence in the profession, such standards for accreditation are as yet not applied to translator education programs. However, if the profession for which they train students is to be recognized as such, the issue of accreditation in translator education in the U.S. urgently needs to be further examined and dealt with despite certain opposition from both academia and practicing translators.

The control maintained by a full-fledged profession over the distinct services it provides for the public is closely related to and derives from the definitional feature of the unique knowledge which distinguishes a profession from a nonprofessional occupation. It therefore keeps non-members from engaging in its professional activities, exerting what for practical purposes must be called a monopoly. How poorly the translator profession fares in this regard and why, when compared to other true professions, becomes even more obvious when we realize that the most fundamental criterion of professionalism, that of possessing a body of specialized knowledge, is indeed the hallmark of the translator profession. However, the claim that this knowledge is shared only by duly certified members of the profession, a factor even more important than the intellectual quality of this knowledge, cannot be made by U.S. translators. In view of the fact that U.S. society associates specialized learned knowledge with university education, it would more readily accept the claim that only members of the translating profession are able to perform competently its distinctive services if the *métier* of a translator were sanctioned by a university degree. Additionally, it would be more willing to grant translators the professional status they merit together with the prestige and salaries commensurate with the importance of their service. I find it, therefore, ironic that the very same reasons why the role of the university in the professionalization of translators is still embattled—namely, the presence in the field of many autodidacts who dispute the necessity of a university training program and the lack of any official regulatory mechanisms in the discipline—may also account for the fact that the translating activity, even though called a profession, does not enjoy the essential rights and responsibilities that constitute membership in a profession in the full sense. Were translating recognized as an equal member among full-fledged professions and translators granted full professional status, they would have the esteem and the financial and other rewards that society so willingly grants to the other professions. If the key factor of a learned profession is a university degree with everything it implies, a curriculum designed and taught by members of the profession actually "professing" in the discipline, then the role of the university in the professionalization of the translator should no longer be subject to controversy.

Another of the university's functions in the professionalization of the translator is to serve as facilitator for continued learning. The dizzying advance of knowledge in all fields of human endeavor makes continued learning a necessity for any professional. The university is the ideal place where experts and scholars can gather at workshops, seminars and conferences to share their insights with students and members of the profession alike. At George Mason University, for example, the annual professional development seminar, sponsored jointly by the local ATA chapter and the university's Translation Program of the Department of Foreign Languages and Literatures, represents a successful attempt at drawing the worlds of academe and the practicing translator together for mutual benefits.

Recognizing the benefits that will result from a closer and, in my view, necessary collaboration of the two worlds for future members of the profession as well as for the profession itself, members should actively strive to improve and support this instrument of professionalization.

NOTES

[1] The statistics gathered by William M. Park list the university based translation programs in the U.S. *Translator and Interpreter Training in the U.S.: A Survey.* Rev. ed. Ossining, NY: ATA, 1990.

In 1983 already, ATA conducted a survey on translator training programs in the U.S. which served as a base for another survey conducted by TRIP at SUNY-Binghamton and reported on by Gabriela Muñoz Mahn: "Current and Desired Status of U.S. Translator Training: Report on 1984 Survey," in *Translation Perspectives II* Selected Papers, 1984-85, ed. Marilyn Gaddis Rose, SUNY-Binghamton, 1985.

[2] Koller, Werner. *Einführung in die Übersetzungswissenschaft.* Quelle & Meyer: Heidelberg, 1979, p. 41.

[3] Edgar Faure in *"La Traduction et l'Université,"* Deuxième Partie, Babel, vol. VIII, No. 3, 1962, p. 121.

[4] A sound pedagogical program has been described by Maier, Carol and Françoise Massardier-Kenney in "How to Ask the Right Questions or, the Pedagogy of Specialized Translation at the Graduate Level." *Looking Ahead, Proceedings of the 31st Annual Conference of the American Translators Association.* Ed. Leslie Willson. Medford, NJ: Learned Information, Inc., 1990, pp. 371-79.

[5] Newmark, Peter. *Approaches to Translation*, Pergamon Press: Oxford, 1981, p. 19.

[6] Krawutschke, Peter W. "The Proposed ATA Program Accreditation." *ATA Series*, vol. 1 (Binghamton, 1987), pp. 30-43.

Krawutschke has worked for many years with academic translation programs. I refer to another excellent article by him: "Translation as an Academic Discipline: Opportunities and Dangers for the Profession." *Proceedings of the 25th Annual Conference of the American Translators Association.* Ed. Patricia E. Newman. Medford, NJ: Learned Information, Inc. 1984.

Ingredients to Success
As a Language Specialist

MARGARETA BOWEN

In discussing success as a language specialist we shall look at multilingualism, natural translation, language studies, world knowledge, university programs, personality, and job satisfaction. Entering the profession—be it as a translator or as an interpreter—may be carefully planned or fortuitous. This applies to multilingualism as well as learning the processes and skills that set translation and interpretation apart from merely being fluent in two or more languages. Furthermore, translating and interpreting comprise various sub-groups of activities calling for different qualities, knowledge, and skills.

Ingredients alone do not make a recipe. How to combine them and in what quantities is as much a matter to decide for the individual, depending on personal circumstances and goals, as is the choice of activity within the language professions. Today language services take many forms and fill many needs.

Multilingualism

Foreign languages are seldom acquired or learned from the beginning with a clear plan in mind, although in public discussions the question is sometimes raised, "If I want to give my child the best preparation possible to become an interpreter, when should he or she start learning which language?" Far more frequently, children happen to be raised in a bilingual environment, go to school in different countries and language communities because of the parents' professions, or distinguish themselves in languages in school and college. More often, a combination of these factors plays a role.

Natural Translation

Undoubtedly, a natural propensity for translating or interpreting exists in some individuals. Harris and Sherwood have described "natural translation" as "[...] the translation done by bilinguals in everyday circumstances and without special training for it." According to them, a bilingual's translation competence develops in parallel with competence in the two languages, from early childhood on, and increases automatically as the child's ability to use the two languages develops. Does this mean that all people who consider themselves bilingual have developed this ability?

The history of the profession tells us about self-made translators and interpreters. Usually only the success stories are passed on for others to admire. And we are not always told about the quality of the service rendered. In the more recent cases we are, when the persons in question worked for an international organization, when their work was printed, when they were awarded prizes. Edouard Roditi and Ewald Osers are examples. A closer look at sources, however, reveals quite a number of non-success stories: Col. Bonsall (23), President Wilson's interpreter at the Preparatory Commission for the Paris Peace talks, relates the case of "a young professor of high attainments and also excellent French" who was so awed by the illustrious statesmen around the conference table that he was unable to produce coherent speech; after one evening he was relieved of the task at the unanimous request of the delegates. Irena Dobosz tells of "several persons [who] were brought from Warsaw and Prague to Panmunjom to try to work at the conference table. Their English and Russian were perfect and yet they couldn't do it. They mumbled, they got confused and lost the thread, they never finished their sentences, they sweated and stammered. It was painful to look at them" (Bowen 1990:31). Ekvall (46) describes the work of the Korean armistice commission, when Army files were searched for people with a thorough knowledge of Korean: "They were men who on their records were rated as qualified linguists. We found most such ratings fictitious. Using practical rule-of-thumb tests, we sent them back—at least four out of every five—as fast as they came." The quote, "But sir, I knew the words, all the words. I just couldn't say them" describes the most dismal failure in Ekvall's book (71-73), an Army captain who was "completely bilingual."

Comprehensive studies to quantify success or failure of natural translation, however, are lacking. Statistics, such as they exist, are incomplete, because the populations investigated are only segments of the total picture. The ad-hoc interpreters who were recruited from among the immigrant population of Somalis to be sent on mission with the U.S. Marines would be an interesting sample to study, but given the circumstances of their service, any reliable follow-up seems unlikely. What we have to go by are figures from professional organizations and the occasional dissertation on the subject (see below). For conference interpreters, AIIC (International Association of Conference Interpreters) has collected statistics showing that a growing number of its members have studied interpreting in specialized courses at a university (72% of the membership in 1984). If the same study were done for full-time translators working for the intergovernmental organizations, the number of people without classroom training in translation would certainly be lower, although all of them would hold a university degree (a condition for employment in most organizations). The U.S. Office of Federal Courts, for its testing program, does not record information about the schooling of candidates, but the success rate of the population tested, in writing and orally, is very low (7.7% in 1980, the first time the test was administered, around 10-12% during the following cycles, and 24% in 1989). Christopher Thiery's thesis on True Bilingualism (*Le bilinguisme chez les interprètes de conférence*) is based on the premise that true bilinguals have acquired their two languages, neither of them serving as a medium of instruction for the other, before puberty. To use these languages professionally, a conscious effort is necessary to keep them at the same level and to update them constantly. Opinions and experience on the appropriate age for training, for both language training and for professional training, vary. A distinction must be made between the proper age for learning languages and the age for preparing specifically for a language profession.

Language Study

Although there is a plethora of publications on the "critical age" for acquiring language proficiency, there is no solid agreement among language teachers. David and Margareta Bowen have discussed the literature in the field (1984). As oral proficiency and communicative skills are considered of paramount importance today, language learning at an early age continues to be seen as a desirable goal, starting in grade school or sometimes in kindergarten. It is true that many young children acquire the sound pattern of a foreign language more easily than adolescents or adults, but individual variations are considerable. For the translator, however, oral proficiency is not indispensable, while comprehension and subject knowledge are essential. For the interpreter who wants to be versatile, all three count. For those interpreters who work from several languages into their mother tongue only, the accent they may have in their foreign languages is not an issue.

Generally, with outstanding capabilities in the mother tongue, the language specialist needs a thorough grounding in the grammar and vocabulary of the foreign languages he or she works with. Danica Seleskovitch has gone on record stating that simultaneous interpreters must have an "intuitive" knowledge of the languages they work with. But this reference to intuition does not concern the way in which foreign languages are learned, nor does it mean that the learning process must have been painless, although a compound bilingual will have this "intuitive" knowledge of two languages to start with. What is essential is the outcome of the learning process, i.e., that the translator or the interpreter does not constantly have to stop and worry about genders, declensions, and conjugations to determine who does what, and to whom. People who had to study their foreign languages can reach the point where they do not have to hesitate to figure out whether *der Tränen* is a masculine singular nominative or a feminine plural genitive noun, like the puzzled graduate student when confronted by the phrase *der Tränen heisse Flut* from a poem by Ringelnatz. In other words, candidates for translating and interpreting must have internalized their working languages sufficiently to survive the short turn-around times which are common in business today and the speed of simultaneous interpreting. Psychologists contrast "effortful" with automatic processing. For interpreters, the term "automatic" used to infuriate them like a red rag waved in front of a bull. A gradual change in attitude seems to be coming about, but as recently as 1986, Else Nowak-Lehmann's presentation at the Trieste Symposium was received with skepticism and disapproval because she mentioned automatic processes, i.e., cognitive processes without conscious cognitive effort. Robert Lado (39) framed his explanation differently when he stated, "Learning a second language involves acquiring varying degrees of facility [...]. These facilities must be learned so that they can operate when attention is on the content and the thread of the argument and not on the expression items."

World Knowledge

In recent years, culture and general knowledge have been incorporated in language courses. Textbooks, tape recordings, videotapes, interactive programs, all have the aim of combining language instruction with information about the culture of the communities whose language is being studied. These courses usually concentrate on the discourse level of the young people learning the language, which is natural and undoubtedly contributes to motivation. Yale University's video series "French in Action" may serve as an example. From the conversations between young Americans in Paris and their French peers, however, it is a great leap to engineers, scientists, and parliamentarians writing reports, talking to each other, and presenting papers at specialized conferences.

Generally, it has been found that even advanced language learners at the college level do not easily refer to the general information they have in order to solve what they perceive as a language problem. The statement that a language is inseparable from its culture is easily accepted, but its implications are not so readily recognized. By "culture" we mean more than the national or regional idiosyncrasies, allusions to literary texts, slang expressions, or references to history. World events and our reactions to them influence the languages we speak, leading to new concepts and hence to new expressions. Two examples may illustrate the language students' difficulty.

At a session of entrance examinations held at Georgetown University, the Spanish text selected had the clause "... *las disposiciones de la Carta de las Naciones Unidas.*" Not one, but several candidates, rendered it as "... the dispositions of the letter of the United Nations." The backgrounds of our candidates vary, but almost all of them had been admitted to a college, usually a selective one; most have a Bachelor's and some a graduate degree. Even this small fragment of a Spanish text held two distinct problems for the candidates. Undoubtedly, one of the first lessons in anyone's Spanish course would include the word *la carta*/the *letter*, as in "Let's write a letter to a friend in Spain." But anyone in the candidates' age group would also have heard at some time about the basic document of the United Nations, the Charter. Had this piece of information been forgotten, or did the candidates just fail to associate it with *la Carta de las Naciones Unidas?* The other problem, *disposiciones*, is more of a language problem, because the term is specific to resolutions and similar texts.

The German text below, from the periodical *Profil*, was presented to a survey class of German Literature during Spring Term 1991 and to one of several sections of an intermediate language class.

> Die USA sind das Land, das Europa die <u>Trennung von Kirche und Staat</u> <u>vorgelebt hat und noch immer vorlebt</u>. Trotzdem findet sich in Europa—Polen und Irland vielleicht ausgenommen—kein Land, in dem Religion so sehr den Alltag, auch den Alltag der Politik beherrscht. Ein Politologe hat sich einmal die Mühe gemacht, auszuzählen, wie oft bestimmte <u>amerikanische Politiker in ihren Reden Gott beschwören</u>—er ist auf (für Europäer) erstaunliche Dimensionen gekommen. Ein wenig <u>erinnert das an Stalin-Zitate kommunistischer Politiker</u> um 1950; oder <u>an Marx-Zitate mancher Sozialwissenschafter</u> um 1970.
>
> Das entspricht durchaus dem religiösen Empfinden der US-Gesellschaft, die zu den religiösesten der Welt zählt. Untersuchungen zeigen, daß neun von zehn Amerikanern noch nie an der Existenz Gottes <u>gezweifelt</u> haben; daß acht von zehn damit rechnen, <u>nach dem Tod ein Jüngstes Gericht</u> zu erleben; daß ebenso viele davon überzeugt sind, Gott würde auch heute noch Wunder wirken.

This test was part of a stratified study we carried out under the terms of a National Resource Center grant from the U.S. Department of Education to determine how well undergraduates were prepared to start advanced translation studies. After eliminating the work of graduate students and those whose questionnaires were incomplete, a sample of 22 undergraduates who worked with this text remained: 14 in the literature class (most of them juniors and seniors, i.e., expecting to graduate in May 1991 or 1992) and eight in an advanced language class (first and second year students).

The best rendition, and the only one of this quality, was the following:

> The U.S. is the nation which has served as a model for Europe—and still does to this day—for the separation of church and state. Despite this there is no European nation (with the possible exceptions of Poland and Ireland) where religion dominates daily life as much, even politics. A political scientist tried one time to count how often certain American politicians use God's name in their speeches—for European standards his results reached amazing dimensions. This is slightly reminiscent of the many references to Stalin's words by communist politicians around 1959 or the quoting of Marx by some social scientists around 1970.

These findings correspond easily to American society's religious consciousness, which is among the most religious in the world. Research shows that 9 out of 10 Americans have never doubted the existence of God, and that eight out of ten expect final judgement after death. Research also shows that just as many are convinced that God would work wonders even in today's world.

Most students in this group had difficulties with *vorleben, beschwören,* and *Jüngstes Gericht. Vorleben* led to: *The USA is one country in which the ideas of church and state has existed and still exist,* or ... *America is the land that divides Church and state, and Europe has increasingly followed the same path* or ... *The United States is the country which was shaped by and continues to be shaped by the separation of church and state in Europe.* In ihren Reden Gott beschwören was rendered as ... *make appeal to God in their speeches,* ... *use God to reinforce their speeches,* ... *swore to God,* ... *mentioned God in their speeches,* and ... *used God's name in vain.*

None of the examples involve simple language problems, although verbs with prefixes are notoriously difficult for learners of German. Neither for *vorleben* nor for *beschwören* would students have found a solution tailored to this text in the dictionaries they usually consult. But these are precisely the instances where making inferences from existing knowledge is called for. For the clause in which *vorleben* is the key verb, considering that the American Constitution and the principle of separation of church and state are part of the high school curriculum, students should have been able to take the clue and connect it with what they know from history and civics courses (both obligatory for college admission). The mention of American politicians' speeches should have been clear to anyone following the news on radio or television. The term *Jüngstes Gericht* may have been unfamiliar to most students who had their religious instruction in English, but the concept should be clear to a predominantly Catholic student body.

The text, like the Italian one used for a previous study by David Bowen et al., deals with the students' own culture, albeit from the point of view of a European. Our collection of examples from different populations, ranging from the unprepared student, who may be a chemistry major, to published translators, shows that getting a message across from one language to another requires an equilibrium of language knowledge and world knowledge. From the handwritten translations furnished for the stratified study, which involved several schools of Georgetown University's main campus, it is clear that many students kept trying to find a verb for the critical verb in the original, over and over again, but did not look at the text as a whole. Texts make sense to their authors, and it is this sense that must come through in the target language for readers or listeners from another culture. If the students in our two groups translating the text on the separation between church and the state were to take up translation studies, most of them would need to learn how to use the factual knowledge they have, together with what they have learned of the language.

Subject Specialization

The ATA Translation Studies Committee has repeatedly dealt with this topic. All concerned agree with the desirability of subject specialization, but when it comes to listing appropriate courses, it is soon discovered that nothing but years of study will suit. Universities plan their curricula for people who want to become lawyers, doctors, or engineers, so usually the decision would be all or nothing. Detailed curriculum design for translation studies with subject specialization, in this author's opinion, will be doomed to failure as long as the American secondary school system provides only for a minimum of foreign language instruction, and usually on a voluntary basis. Eight years of a foreign language in secondary school, as is the practice in the German and Austrian system, does not necessarily provide for an unlimited pool of candidates, but the eight years allow teachers and students to progress far enough for talent to declare itself. The young people, therefore, have a better basis for choosing a curriculum, and translation studies can start at a higher level, incorporating more background courses. As to the marketability of strict subject specialization, ATA members continue to report their pessimism, especially when these members have a narrow language specialization as well, e.g., Russian into English. Research skills and a network of sources, including engineers who work as engineers, chemists working as chemists, etc., as described by William H. Skinner in the *Jerome Quarterly*, and by authors elsewhere in this volume appear to give better results.

Personal Qualities

The first generation of conference interpreters maintained that interpreting was an innate skill; "interpreters (or translators) are born, not made," was the generally accepted theory; some said that interpreters have an extra gyrus in their brain. By now, several generations of conference interpreters have proved that interpreting can be learned. As in the case of many other professions, certain qualities are necessary or desirable from the outset, while others can be acquired. Recently, a graduate student about to pick a subject for his thesis asked, "What is the personality profile of an interpreter?" Various publishers of career information have tried to answer this question. Usually they come up with "the translator is an introvert" and "the interpreter is an extrovert," or "the interpreter has to be aggressive." These are considered innate traits. Memory is also sometimes listed as such a trait. Patricia Longley mentions André Kaminker's ability to read a page from a telephone directory and retain every name on it and repeat every name in the right order; among the author's colleagues was one who knew the departure times of all the major trains out of Vienna by heart. Today, many authors talk about "memory training."

Let us beware of oversimplifications. Mnemonic techniques were developed to a high degree for societies without books or a low literacy rate. These techniques make for fascinating studies in rhetoric and literature, but they hardly ever work for practical situations in today's world. How often has anyone had to translate a page from the telephone directory without looking at it? The introvert translator would have a hard time dealing with clients and the extrovert interpreter is certain to find social contacts at work rather restricted.

Among the main characteristics for the language professional I would list a certain adaptability—to different cultures, for a start, to different situations, different clients, different colleagues. An ability to concentrate and to use all intellectual resources and to compensate for weaknesses is very important. Personal integrity is a requirement, as it is for any profession. Moreover, on a more practical level, professionals need some business sense, the ability to control their finances (which has little to do with how much you earn—as described by Helen Gurley Brown in her now otherwise dated books) and punctuality.

University Programs

As Roditi stated in an outreach paper on the history of the profession, originally interpreters often were from border regions and of mixed parentage. Immigrants to the U.S. often fill a gap in the language professions.

Their education may not have been completed in any one country. But even if many practicing translators and interpreters were able to start without any specific preparation, they increasingly feel the need for further education.

A university degree is required for employment by most intergovernmental organizations and many government agencies. The freelance professional has no such requirement, as long as he or she offers quality performance. But having relevant degrees, certificates, recommendations from colleagues or clients, membership in professional organizations, all contribute to convincing prospective clients that the service provided will have been worth contracting for.

Looking for a common denominator would be difficult, since the professional organizations all have a multinational membership. It is safe to state, however, that the number of university-educated translators and interpreters has been steadily growing in most countries. This is not only true for Western Europe and the United States, but also for Latin America and Australia, Russia, the new Republics, and many Asian and African countries.

The ATA list of university programs and courses shows the diversity of approaches, designed to suit different needs: general translation, technical translation, terminology and computer-aided translation, community interpreting, escort interpreting, court interpreting, and conference interpreting. Young people who get drawn to translation studies by their interest in foreign languages can now plan their course of action, depending on how high they wish to set their goals and how much time they can devote to studying. A specific example, that of the institution where the author teaches, will serve as an example of what a university course can offer.

Georgetown University has been training generalist translators and conference interpreters since 1949. It continues to be one of the most concentrated courses of study in the U.S. and elsewhere, which means applicants have to be screened very carefully. Changes have come about under the impetus of market changes and today's program is quite different from what it was in the beginning. The University was helped through various grants, notably the National Resource Center grant from the U.S. Department of Education which it shared with the State University of New York at Binghamton from 1981 to 1991.

What are these changes? First, courses providing for translation from and into the foreign language taught by the same teacher to the same students were phased out, and a number of combinations from the foreign language into English were added (Portuguese into English, Italian into English). More specialized material is used in all courses, e.g., papers on medical topics, the environment, agriculture, and energy. All technical equipment has been updated repeatedly; interpreting students use actual conference equipment for simultaneous exercises; student performance in public speaking and consecutive interpreting is video-recorded and a collection of videotapes furnishes a variety of speakers, accents, and subjects for exercises. With the guidance of experienced conference interpreters, students reach a point where, once they have started working, we can say "after this course of studies, no matter how difficult a meeting you are assigned to, you have experienced it before in the classroom."

Several years ago introductory courses to translation and interpreting were added to Georgetown University's program. These courses are available without an entrance examination and are geared to acquainting the students with the general principles of professional work while providing exercises to put these principles into practice. All exercises take place in English, in consecutive. Undergraduates taking these courses are in a better position to evaluate their status and prospects. Prospective community interpreters with languages unavailable in any advanced program are able to prepare for badly needed service.

Job Satisfaction or How to Tell Success

Job satisfaction is an obvious manifestation of success. When talking to former students about their work, we invariably ask them "If you had to do it all over again, would you?" The answer has been in the affirmative in most cases. Some have changed careers, often for family reasons or because some other interest came to the fore. The hallmark of a successful freelance is a certain margin of choice, a variety of clients, most of them faithful, just as an employee should not feel locked in with one employer.

REFERENCES

AIIC Bulletin XII:1, March 1984, p. 25.
Bonsall, Stephen. *Unfinished Business.* Garden City, NJ: Doubleday & Co. Inc., 1944.
Botkin, James W., Mahdi Elmandjra and Mircea Malitza. *No Limits to Learning. Bridging the Human Gap. A Report to the Club of Rome.* Oxford, New York, Toronto, Sydney, Paris, Frankfurt: Pergamon Press, 1979.

Bowen, David. *The Intercultural Component in Interpreter and Translator Training: A Historical survey.* Unpublished doctoral dissertation (Georgetown Univ.: Washington, D.C., 1985).

Bowen, David et al. "Italian into English Translation Evaluation and Comparison," *The Jerome Quarterly*, 3:3, May-June 1988, pp. 7-10.

Bowen, David and Margareta. "The Results to be Expected from a Stay Abroad." Wilss Wolfram and Gisela Thome, eds., *Translation Theory and its Implementation in the Teaching of Translating and Interpreting.* Tübingen: Gunter Narr Verlag, 1984, pp. 279-88.

Bowen, David and Margareta. *Interpreting—Yesterday, Today and Tomorrow.* ATA Series, vol. 4. Binghamton: State University of New York at Binghamton. 1990.

Bowen, Margareta. "Bilingualism as a Factor in Translation and Interpretation." James E. Alatis, ed., *Current Issues in Bilingual Education.* Washington, D.C.: Georgetown Univ. Press, 1980.

Bowen, Margareta. "Language Learning and Becoming a Professional Translator." *The Jerome Quarterly*, 4:4, Washington, D.C.: National Resource Center for Translation and Interpretation, Aug.-Sept. 1989, pp. 2, 10-11.

Dollerup, Cay and Anne Loddegaard, eds. *Teaching Translation and Interpreting. Training, Talent and Experience.* Amsterdam/Philadelphia: John Benjamins Publishing Company, 1992.

Ekvall, Robert B. *Faithful Echo.* New York: Twayne Publishers, 1960.

Harris, Brian and Bianca Sherwood. "Translation as an Innate Skill." *Language Interpretation and Communication.* Ed. Gerver D. and H. W. Sinaiko. New York and London: Plenum Press, 1978. 155-70.

de Jongh, Elena M. *An Introduction to Court Interpreting: Theory and Practice.* Lanham, New York, London: University Press of America, 1992.

Longley, Patricia E. *Conference Interpreting.* London: Sir Isaac Pitman & Sons Ltd., 1968.

Lado, Robert. *Language Teaching, a Scientific Approach.* New York, San Francisco, Toronto, London: McGraw-Hill, 1964.

Newman, Patricia. "The Second Step." *The Jerome Quarterly*, 4:2. Washington, D.C.: National Resource Center for Translation and Interpretation, Feb.-March 1989, pp. 2, 13.

Roditi, Edouard. "The History of Interpretation in a Nutshell." Washington, D.C.: National Resource Center for Translation and Interpretation, 1982.

Skinner, William. "On Reaching the First Million (Words)." *The Jerome Quarterly*, 6:3, May-June 1991, pp. 3-5, 10.

Thiery, Christopher. *Le bilinguisme chez les interprètes de conférence.* Doctoral thesis: Sorbonne Nouvelle, Paris III, 1975.

Non-Discriminatory Approaches in Translation Studies

DAVID BOWEN

In his autobiographical work Vernon Walters mentions a letter of thanks from President Eisenhower "Before I leave the White House [...] The service you rendered me over a long period of time was invaluable—not only because you are so expert in the various languages at your command, but also because of your intelligent grasp of the problems and background of the various countries we together visited."

The first international organizations to employ conference interpreters and to set up professional translation services were predominantly organizations of European countries, e.g., the League of Nations, the International Labor Office, the International Red Cross. Between 1920 and 1945 interpretation was used mainly between delegates who shared a common Greco-Roman/Judeo-Christian heritage. Scientists attending non-governmental conferences had gone to one of a limited number of universities in Europe or the United States. Cultural contrasts were due to differences in political aims and systems, and differences between generations, not to profound cultural contrasts.

The United Nations, when the organization came into being after World War II, at first, had a limited membership, mostly the developed nations. The war-ravaged European countries' first concern was avoiding future wars. The newly independent countries, as they gradually were released from trusteeship and colonial status and became full-fledged members, were keenly aware of the "other" traditions of what, often, had been their colonizers. Gradually, they asserted themselves.

Today, employers have become as diversified as the modern world, encompassing international organizations with a claim to universality, first and foremost the United Nations family of organizations, then regional organizations of varying size, e.g., the Pan-American Organizations, and professional organizations, e.g., international labor union federations. Even the political organizations become involved in development and environmental issues and have to deal with more and more technical material. The volume of translations has been growing in direct proportion to the efforts of inter-African and international cooperation involving countries other than the former colonizers. The regional organizations, e.g., the Organization of African Unity (founded in 1963), the League of Arab States (founded in 1945), the Organization of Petroleum Exporting Countries (founded in 1960), and the Caribbean Community (founded in 1973) are creating a tradition of their own. In Asia and Australia, the growing economic importance of the Pacific Rim countries led to increased demand for translation and interpretation in languages hitherto considered irrelevant in international relations. The oil crisis solidly established Arabic, and to some extent Farsi, as conference languages. Farsi also had to be used in some cases before the International Court of Justice after the fall of the Shah. The consequences of the breakup of the Soviet Union have yet to be evaluated; at present U.S. institutions seem to be in a rush toward creating new courses in Ukrainian and the languages of Eastern Europe. It is only natural that the new players in international politics would want to participate in the training of professionals for a service which can be of crucial importance to the countries involved. Since the late sixties and early seventies, the newly independent nations of Africa have felt a growing need for the services of highly qualified, professionally trained African conference interpreters. They no longer wish to import them from Europe or elsewhere. The same is true for most other countries. This has led to the founding of a number of schools for translators and interpreters all over the world, and it also has led to the need of giving students anywhere a broad cultural background that is not limited to the European or American traditions. Most employers of translators and interpreters, even if only the "classical" conference languages are to be used, expect these professionals to have a broad cultural background and to be aware of global concerns.

Until the founding of the Buea School in Cameroon, there was no training facility for sub-Saharan Africa. Candidates had to be sent to either Europe or North America for training. The objective was to select, send, have trained, pass the final exam and return home to help meet the need which had led to the whole exercise in the first place. Usually these students were selected by their own governments and sponsored by them or by other countries and organizations. It was understood that the standards to be applied would be the same for all students. Considering that, for these students, English, French or Portuguese are vehicular languages, imposed from above and school learned, their starting point is not the same as it is for students with one of these languages as a mother tongue. Nevertheless, some of these students have become outstanding professionals. They are now equal partners in the dialogue with their contemporaries and their teachers, and it is they who stress the principle of turnabout is fair play. If they are expected to have the same background as their European and American counterparts, they ask: "What about the awareness of African cultures outside of Africa?" African or Asian names can be quite difficult for Europeans or Americans—so, "learn to pronounce them, we have a hard time with some of yours!" A student who thinks the Alps are a river and the Rhine might be a mountain in Bohemia is laughed at by his or her classmates. But ignorance of the political map of Africa is rampant, as Valentin Ndi Mbro of the International Monetary Fund stated in a lecture to Georgetown students, and it behooves us to remedy this situation.

The Arabic-speaking countries and Iran are just as much aware of the need for training their own translators and interpreters. Beirut University has a well established program for translators and interpreters, while the *Ecole Supérieure Roi Fahd de Traduction* in Tangiers is the most recent addition to the number of programs and courses in various Arabic-speaking countries. Iranian programs are regularly represented at European conferences, e.g., the Elsinore Conference on the teaching of translation and interpreting and the Vienna conference on translation studies (1992). The ESIT (*Ecole Supérieure de Traduction et d'Interprétation* at the Sorbonne Nouvelle, University of Paris), which has been offering special programs for Arabic, Korean, Japanese and Chinese interpreters for many years, also is the only institution currently offering a doctorate in the science of translation and interpretation. Several theses have been written on the cultural elements that have been recognized as being of pervading importance for translation studies, e.g., on the translations of *Arabian Nights* into French.

How do teaching institutions incorporate this wide spectrum of cultural knowledge into their coursework? Can U.S. institutions follow the example of schools in other countries? The typical four-year program at European universities offers area studies as a complement to language study in a common track before students take up translation studies proper. Even with the traditional conference languages, e.g., French, English and German, and concentrating mainly on European cultures, this has been a tall order.

As an example, let us look at the list of courses offered in "*Landes- und Kulturkunde*" at the University of Vienna, Institute for Translator and Interpreter Training: Under this rubric, a total of 85 credits was offered for Fall Term 1992, covering Czech (6 CR), English (16), French (14 CR), German (8 CR), Hungarian (6 CR), Italian (8 CR), Polish (4 CR), Portuguese (6 CR), Rumanian (2 CR), Russian (4 CR), Serbo-croat (4 CR), and Spanish (7 CR). These area courses are mainly overviews of art, literature, geopolitics and the press. Many are part of a two- or three-semester sequence. To keep things in proportion, it should be added that the Institute has about 5,000 students, who begin their four-year plus course of studies normally after leaving high school. Until age 27, Austrian citizens do not pay any tuition for higher education. For Western Europe, the situation at the University of Vienna is not atypical, although, of course, there are differences. Much depends on the offerings of other departments, which are cross-listed or generally accessible to students, e.g., at the University of Heidelberg course titles such as "The Third Republic" (France), "The French Novel in the 19th Century, III," "British Life and Letters, Part II: Restoration and Eighteenth Century," "American Naturalism," "American History from the Civil War to World War I," "L'actualité politique, économique et sociale en France (émissions télé et autres médias)." French and English are most often represented in students' language combinations, hence a considerable breadth of offerings. For the less frequently represented languages (i.e., languages not normally taught in European secondary schools), such as Spanish and Portuguese, there is usually just one course on this level. The former Maurice Thorez Institute's school for interpreters in Moscow, now reorganized within the Moscow Linguistic University, offers a similar program.

If we compare this situation to a one- or two-year course of studies, which is not uncommon in the United States, several caveats are in order: age, admission policies, and course titles. For a one- or two-year program, applicants either have a bachelor's degree, sometimes a graduate or a professional degree, or they have relevant work experience. They are more mature in either case. U.S. universities generally screen their applicants and the top institutions admit only a small percentage of their applicant pool. Finally, course titles usually name only the practical exercises to be gone through, i.e., advanced translation for specific language combinations, consecutive or simultaneous interpreting, public speaking, etc. This leaves a great deal of flexibility in the material to be used for these exercises to suit the particular year's student group.

Georgetown University's Division of Interpretation and Translation traditionally has an international student group. Candidates are screened by entrance examinations in their language combinations before they are admitted to the course. The Division faculty's work on this testing has been published extensively in the U.S. and abroad. The advanced courses, in a two-semester sequence, lead directly to examinations for professional translators/interpreters. The prerequisites which must be taken before admission are courses in international relations, business, philosophy, history and literature; they answer the need for "shared information" on the part of the translator, i.e., the intercultural component that is even more important than subject specialization. In the United States, language and area studies frequently leave no time in the curriculum for a second or third language. Both in the choice of material for exercises and the choice of prerequisite courses, students are directed towards areas they have not studied before, e.g., an African student may be directed to take a course on Greek and Roman history, an American to a course on francophone Africa. As one of the division's lecturers points out in her Orientation Institute lecture: "You must read newspapers, and read those sections that you would normally skip!"

For the coursework's exercises, topics are carefully selected, e.g., for public speaking assignments. A collection of videotaped speeches by students from many different countries of the world on a variety of topics has thus been built up over the years, and is complemented by guest lectures. Extracurricular course enhancement ranges from specific events initiated by the Division, usually visits of colleagues, main campus events and lecture series, such as "Islamism and Secularism in North Africa" offered free of charge for Georgetown students by the Center of Contemporary Arab Studies, to the many opportunities offered by the international environment in the nation's capital. Faculty has been building up a collection of catalogs and slides of art exhibits covering many cultures, e.g., the Benin bronzes of Africa, the Kyoto Moss Garden (now closed to the public), the Italian Renaissance and others. Art collecting and art robbery are topics of discussion in the context of international treaties protecting the signatory countries' cultural heritage. A further source of cultural variety is the SCOLA program, as described by Jacqueline Tanner (2). For 10 years,

SCOLA has brought TV News from about 40 countries to schools and colleges across the United States via satellite. For five years the channel has been operating 24 hours a day, every day of the year. It covers international and area studies, business and other disciplines. The Division has an installation in its interpreter training facility, where the program can be fed directly into the simultaneous interpreting system for student practice. The SCOLA STARS project, now in the proposal stage, intends to bring foreign mathematics, science and language classes (e.g., the languages of Eastern Europe, Portuguese, Greek, Swahili and others) to American schools.

John B. Carroll's (3) statement that "The test maker is not concerned with how well the examinee comprehends a *particular* spoken or written text; rather, he is concerned with the examinee's ability to comprehend a sample of such texts, in order to infer the examinee's ability to understand additional texts," applies to all translation teaching. We do not train people to translate a finite number of specific texts, but our students should be able to solve the problems of a wide range of texts, including references to many cultures, even those not directly related to their working languages. The increasing use of relay for some of the newly added conference languages reinforces this need. Carroll adds (3) "Comprehension ability tests tend to be substantially correlated with 'intelligence' tests, even those of a nonverbal character, [...] one possible source of this correlation is the fact that reading and listening comprehension tests do not measure *only* what may be called 'pure' comprehension of language; because of the way in which they are constructed, and the kind of items they include, they tend also to measure ability to make inferences and deductions from text content."

Each student is expected to submit during the course a paper on metaphors, proverbs, and cultural innuendo. Research skills are honed by students' using existing documentation such as bilateral and multilateral agreements on cultural relations, and developing the ability to perform self-directed research using our rich library resources. The most important step, however, is for the student to learn how to use the acquired background knowledge when translating, as illustrated by the example given by M. Bowen in this volume (the German/English test administered to a random population of undergraduates). How do the two approaches, the four-year program with specific culture courses, and the one- or two-year program, compare? The time at which the student makes a commitment to translation studies is much earlier in the four-year program area studies, and the advantage of more hours for background courses must be weighed against the increasing difficulty of changing career orientation in the course of the four or more years. Students applying to the shorter programs after four years in college usually have made their career choice better informed and more aware of their strengths and weaknesses. As they are more mature, they are usually able to face the concentrated, intensive work. "*Landeskunde*" in the typical four-years plus programs of institutions in Western Europe give more details that can possibly be furnished in a shorter program, but some of these courses, especially if they are part of the program for a different major, are becoming too specialized for the requirements of today's marketplace. While courses listed for literature majors can be useful as background courses for translation and interpretation students, institutional structures in the U.S. often are too rigid to allow for joint planning.

We are aware that many members of the translation/interpretation profession in the U.S. are of the opinion that literature courses are of little interest to translation studies, considering the prevalence of scientific and technical material. It is true that English writing in this field has little in common with literary style. In the Romance languages, however, the more complicated syntactic structures can be learned through literary texts, where they are more frequent, and provide a solid basis for later work. When correcting student translations, one finds many instances where this basis would have avoided misunderstandings, and helped the student gain time, as in the following example from a recent examination, an article on AIDS: *El carácter de este virus hace que la infección se produzca a través de un sistema de replicación, lo que significa que el linfocito que posee la información del virus no genera virus completo contagioso más que en caso de que se divida al ser estimulado*. The nature of this virus causes the infection to be produced through a system of replication, which means that the lymphocyte that possesses the virus information does not create a complete, contagious virus *even if it is divided into the stimulated being*. The misunderstanding here clearly is due to insufficient knowledge of Spanish syntax, which could have been remedied by the kind of reading that literature courses include.

Obviously, choices must be made, and in different educational systems and different institutions the solutions will be different, and they will be more or less suitable for different student groups and different personalities. In the end, what counts is the result.

REFERENCES

TURJUMAN. Journal of Translation Studies, Université Abdelmalek Essaâdi, *Ecole Supérieure Roi Fahd de Traduction*. Tangiers, Morocco.

Bowen, David and Margareta. "Discourse for Interpreter Training." *The Jerome Quarterly*, 5:4, Aug.-Sept. 1990, pp. 5-7, 10. Washington, D.C.: Georgetown Univ., SLL.

———. "Entrance Examinations for Translation and Interpretation." *ADFL Bulletin*, September 1985.

———. "Aptitude for Interpreting." *Proceedings of the 1st Symposium on the Theoretical and Practical Aspects of Teaching Interpretation*, Laura Gran and John Dodds, eds. Trieste: Univ. of Trieste, 1989.

Carroll, John B. and Roy O. Freedle (eds). Carroll John B. "Defining Language Comprehension," in *Language Comprehension and the Acquisition of Knowledge*. Washington, D.C.: V. H. Winston & Sons, 1972.

Tanner, Jacquelyn. "SCOLA's STAR'S Project." *The Jerome Quarterly*. Vol. 8:1, Nov.-Dec. 1992, p. 2. Washington, D.C.: Georgetown Univ., SLL.

Walters, Vernon A. *Silent Missions*. Garden City, NY: Doubleday and Co., 1978.

The Current Status of U.S. Translator and Interpreter Training

WILLIAM M. PARK

Foreign language teachers in high schools and universities are frequently asked a question they find themselves ill-prepared to answer: "What can I do with foreign languages if I don't want to teach?" A typical answer is "You should be an interpreter at the United Nations," or "There are jobs with the government in Washington." Each of these answers opens the door to more difficult questions: "How can I become an interpreter?" "What's the difference between an interpreter and a translator?" "What are the U.N. qualifications?" "Where in the government are there jobs?" "How do I go about applying?" Language instructors often have little or no experience outside the academic world, and would be unaware of the needs of international business and government. Even worse, because of a pervasive attitude in the educational establishment that translator/interpreter (T&I) training is somehow "vocational" (unlike teacher training, which is accepted as a "pure" university discipline), most language teachers have no idea where T&I programs are being offered in this country—or whether they exist at all.

Turning to professional translators or interpreters for help often accomplishes little. Those who have had the good fortune of receiving training in this country or abroad will probably recommend their alma mater, without really knowing its standing in relation to other institutions. And those who, like myself, could never find the further education they so eagerly sought will be reduced to passing on bits of lore about places mentioned in conversations, talks at conventions or professional publications.

Only one fact is consistent: the "prestigious" universities are noticeably absent, with few exceptions, from any list on T&I training. Institutions which offer T&I programs are generally more innovative, attempting to break away from the comfortable, traditional language and literature degrees that were acceptable in the job market of 50 years ago—and still are, for graduates interested in a teaching career.

For this reason, among others, the Translation Studies Committee of the ATA saw the need to gather information on these newer programs. The first directory of institutions offering T&I training in the U.S. was compiled by Etilvia Arjona in 1981, the second by Marilyn Gaddis Rose in 1983, while each chaired the ATA Translation Studies Committee. The 1989 directory was begun while I chaired the committee, and completed with the support and encouragement of Josephine Thornton, who succeeded me.

While the 1983 directory was thorough in its coverage of the profession, it could not provide the information necessary to advise students on more advanced programs available, or to allow rapid comparison of programs. Essentially all institutions were treated alike, whether they had graduate programs or single courses. In addition, it was not always clear whether the courses themselves were specially designed for T&I training or traditional language courses that included some translation exercises. The hierarchical design of the 1989 and 1993 directories, with the names of the courses listed, should prove more useful in determining which programs are best suited to the student.

Although some three dozen programs of four or more courses (a traditional minimum) now exist in the U.S., they are widely scattered. The likelihood of a program or even a course within commuting distance is remote, outside of certain large population centers with an international outlook, such as New York or Washington. The question is often asked, "Why are there so few programs?" The most obvious answer is that traditional universities, particularly those that have been around a long time, are very timorous about venturing into new fields. Even for more progressive institutions the problem of balancing costs is ever-present: a new translating program may not attract enough students to justify the use of faculty time (interpreting is even less cost-effective, due to the small pool of qualified students). And a further philosophical question emerges: "Should we promote programs involved with translating into English, particularly from the more common languages, in light of the shifting job market?" There may be some justification for translator training programs from English into languages such as Spanish, but these would make sense only in areas with enough native speakers of these languages to provide a pool of local students for the initial years. However, a case could be made for a certain amount of T&I training as a general humanities requirement, because of the components that go into both translating and interpreting (linguistic skill, analysis of information, content knowledge in a variety of fields, decision-making, development of native-language writing/speaking).

The current Survey[1] is based on several assumptions about its audience that have arisen from practice. First, it is unlikely that this information will be available at the high school level, since most high school teachers and counselors are completely unaware of the existence of T&I training. Secondly, those using this Survey are unlikely to be currently enrolled at an institution with suitable T&I courses and/or programs, and would thus have to contemplate a change of institution with all that such a move entails (it is for this reason that the T&I programs have pride of place in the Survey over single courses: no one should seriously consider transferring to another university solely for a single course which may or may not be currently available). Thirdly, the Survey provides only the basic details on each program or course, and it is up to the user to augment these by contacting the appropriate institutions for expanded and updated information, particularly on entrance/exit requirements and next possible date of entry where programs do not begin every semester.

In addition to a table of contents and a geographical index, this list is arranged hierarchically by level of instruction, with the highest degrees first. within each category institutions appear alphabetically. Some offer both programs and individual courses scattered throughout different departments; to avoid fragmentation and allow a clear overview, all T&I training offered by an institution will appear grouped under the highest degree, with a cross-listing for lower-level programs (but not for single courses). The rationale for this is derived from practice: a student interested in a translation program in one language may wish to build up an applied background in another. Showing the entire range of programs and courses in one location allows the student to narrow choices for further study before contacting the appropriate institution(s).

Since there is as yet no agreement on the minimum number of courses constituting a program, I have taken a minimalist approach by defining a program as having at least two courses in a developmental sequence. Eventually a firmer definition of the term "program" will have to be established, as well as criteria for the various degree levels, which in some cases overlap, but this is the function of the ATA University Accreditation Committee. It is hoped that the Survey will aid in the Committee's efforts.

Following the name of each course in most cases is a code indicating a language pair and direction. Single-letter abbreviations are used for Arabic, Chinese, English, French, German, Hebrew, Italian, Japanese, Korean, Portuguese, Russian and Spanish; other languages are spelled out in full. For example, (E>R) means the direction of translation is English to Russian, while (F>G, G>E, S>E) means French-German- or Spanish-to-English. A number after this code denotes the number of hours for the course (in semester hours unless otherwise indicated). Finally, the course emphasis (L=literary or NL=nonliterary) will appear if applicable. While it is understood that both literary and nonliterary texts are used in many cases, emphasis is usually given to one or the other. Where literary and nonliterary texts are used equally, the word "none" appears on the "Emphasis" line. Note that a program with one emphasis may include courses with the other.

For those specifically interested in interpreting, a list of programs may be found at the end of the foreword (the level in parentheses shows the section in which the program is listed and not necessarily the level of interpreting offerings). Some interpreting courses may also be found in the Individual Course section.

This survey was compiled as an ATA service and does not imply endorsement of any institution by the Association, nor is any qualitative rating implied. Information supplied by individual institutions was entered from the questionnaires with only slight editing for format. While it is possible that an existing program somewhere in the country was not listed, it is highly unlikely. Every effort was made to track down rumors of programs that had not been contacted either directly or through the ATA Chronicle. Naturally, I am always happy to hear of new offerings, whether courses or programs. Now that a format has been set up it should be feasible to update the survey every two or three years with relative ease and greater accuracy.

I hope that this brief overview of the T&I training situation in this country will assist students seeking to expand their career options and provide models of successful programs to innovative foreign language departments as they address the difficult process of curriculum development.

NOTE

[1] Park, William M. Translator and Interpreter Training in the USA. A Survey, 2nd ed. Arlington, VA: American Translators Association, 1993. Available from ATA HQ for $10, U.S. postage paid.

Contributors

Bernard Bierman is President of AdEx Translations International, Inc., New York, and Managing Editor of TRANSLATION NEWS.

Gabe Bokor is the owner-manager of Accurapid Translation Services/AB Typesetting in Poughkeepsie, New York.

David Bowen is Associate Professor in the Division of Interpretation and Translation, Georgetown University, Washington, D.C.

Margareta Bowen is Associate Professor and Head of the Division of Interpretation and Translation, Georgetown University, Washington, D.C.

Anne D. Cordero is Associate Professor of French, George Mason University, Fairfax, Virginia, and Director of the Graduate Certificate Program in Translation.

Doris Ganser has had her own translation bureau in Kansas City, Missouri since 1974.

Deanna L. Hammond, ATA past president of ATA and Gode Medal recipient, is head of Language Services of the Congressional Research Service at the Library of Congress, Washington, D.C.

Jane Maier is a freelance translator in Boulder, Colorado.

Alan Melby is Professor of Linguistics and Director of the Translation Research Group, Brigham Young University, Provo, Utah.

Nancy Schweda Nicholson is Associate Professor of Linguistics and Director of the Interpretation Program, University of Delaware, Newark.

William M. Park is Associate Professor of German, Director of Language Laboratories, and Coordinator of the Certificate in Translating Program, University of North Carolina at Charlotte.

Ann C. Sherwin is a freelance translator in Raleigh, North Carolina.

Nancy M. Snyder has been working full time as a freelance translator under the name Technical Language Services since 1988.

John F. Szablya is a consulting engineer and a freelance translator, Bellevue, Washington. He is Professor Emeritus, Washington State University, Pullman, Washington, and Affiliate Professor, University of Washington, Seattle.

Helen M. Szablya is Honorary Consul for Hungary, and a freelance translator, for the States of Washington, Oregon, and Idaho. She and John F. Szablya own and manage a trade consulting company.

Muriel Vasconcellos, formerly chief of translation services at the Pan American Health Organization, Washington, D.C., is a freelance translator and consultant on machine translation.

ATA Corporate/Institutional Members (AS OF 4/12/1993)

A & M Logos International, Inc.
A E Inc., Translations
A L Madrid & Associates
Academy Interpreting and Translations International
Academy of Languages
Academy of Legal and Technical Translations, Ltd.
Accento, The Language Company
Accura International Translations
Accurapid Translation Services, Inc.
Accurate International Translations, Inc.
Accuword International, Inc./Inlingua
Ace Translation Center
AD-EX Worldwide
Adaptive Language Resources, Inc.
Adams Technical Translations, Acs Inc.
Affinity Language Services
Albors and Associates, Inc.
Allen Translation Service
Allied Languages Cooperative
American Bureau of Professional Translators
American Institute of Physics
American Translation Company
Amway Corporation
AN-NAHDA Educational Office
Arccas Interpreting, Inc.
Asia Foreign Language Institute
Asist Translation Services, Inc.

ATA Corporate/Institutional Members

A T & T Language Line
Benemann Translation Center - BTC
Bergen Language Institute, Inc.
Berkeley Scientific Translation Service, Inc.
Bilingual Services
Binghamton University (SUNY)
Biolingua, Incorporated
Bowne Translation Services
Bradson Corporation
Brazilian Translated
Burg Translation Bureau
BYU Translation Eesearch Group
CACI Language Center
Caere Corporation
Calvin International Communications, Inc.
Canadian Union of Professional & Technical Employees
Center for Applied Linguistics
Center for Professional Advancement
Cherry Valley Language Technology
Chicago Multi-lingua Graphics, Inc.
Christian Science Publishing Society
The Church of Jesus Christ of LDS, Translation Dept.
Cincilingua, Inc.
Community Interpreter Services
Community Management Staff
Comnet International
Contact International
Copper Translation Service
Corporate Language Services, Inc.
The Corporate Word, Inc.
Cosmopolitan Translation Bureau
Crimson Language Services
Data General Corporation
Diplomatic Language Services, Inc.
Direct Language Communications
Diversified Language Institute
Document Processing Center, Inc.
Dovali Translation, Inc.
Dynamic Language Center, Ltd.

East-West Concepts, Inc.
Ebon Research System
Eriksen Translations, Inc.
Ers
European Languages Plus
Excelcom/Translex
Federal News Services
FLS, Inc.
Foreign Language Center
G.T. Translation Services, Inc.
Galaxy Systems, Inc.
Gallaudet University
Garjak International, Inc.
Geonexus Communications
Georgetown University
Georgia State University
Gerard Linguistic Services
Glaxo, S.A.
The Global Institute of Languages & Culture, Inc.
Global Language Management
Global Translation Services, Inc.
Globaldoc, Inc.
Globalink, Inc.
Globus Language Communications
GLS International
GM&A International
Grupo Celer-Pawlowsky
Harvard Translations
Hightech Passport
Hispanic Service Center
i.b.d. Ltd.
Iberia Language Services
IBM Corporation
Idem Translation
Infosoft International
Inlingua International Services
Institut Für Fremdsprachen Und Auslandskunde
Instituto Superior de Intérpretes y Traductores, S.A.
Inter-American Air Force Academy/Itak

Intercontact - Peru
Intercultural Communications Inc.
Intergraph Corporation
Interleaf, Inc.
Interlink Communications & Marketing Group, Inc.
Internation Communication, Inc.
International Business Communications Corporation
International Communications, Inc.
International Contact, Inc.
International Communication Network
International Language Engineering Corporation
International Language Services, Inc.
International Word, Inc.
Interpreters International and Translations
Interpreting Services International, Inc.
Iverson Language Associates, Inc.
Jackson Graphics, Inc.
Japan Translation Federation, Inc.
Japanese Language Services, Inc.
Jem Translation Services
JKW Internation, Inc.
JLS
John Benjamins Publishing
Josef Silny & Associates, Inc.
Kien SNC
Koei Corporation
The Language Company
The Language Connection
Language Interface, Ltd.
The Language Lab
Language Link Corporation
Language Matters
Language Plus
The Language Service, Inc.
Language Services International, Ltd.
Languages Unlimited
Laurentian University School of Translators & Interpreters
Lawyers' & Merchants' Translation Bureau, Inc.
Leo Rosenblum & Associates

Lingua Communications Translation Services
Lingua Media, Inc.
Lingualink Incorporated
Linguanet, Inc.
Linguistic Services for Professionals, Inc.
Linguistic Systems, Inc.
Linguistic Translation Service
LINX Interpretation Service
Logos Corporation
M2 Limited
Marygrove College
Master Translating Services, Inc.
Gene Mayer Associates
Mayo Clinic Language Department
Ralph Mcelroy Translation Company
MCS Language Connection
Mellon Bank
Mercury Marine
Mitaka Limited
Morgan Guaranty Trust Company
Multiling International, Inc.
Multilingual Communications Corporation
Multilingual Translations, Inc.
NCS Enterprises, Inc.
New Jersey Department of Corrections, Hispanic Services
New York University
Nichibei International Services
O'Sullivan Menu Corporation
Occidental International Exploration & Production
Omni Interpreting & Translating Network
Omnilingua, Inc.
P.H. Brink International
Pacific Interpreters, Inc.
Pacific Quest Corporation
Pacifica Corporation
Pancom International, Inc.
Peters Translation
Professional Translating Services
Protrans, Inc.

PSC, Inc.
Purdue University
Quantum, Inc.
Rapport International
Reliable Renditions
Rennert Bilingual Translations
Rocky Mountain Translators
Rose-Hulman Institute of Technology
Routledge, Inc.
Sally Low & Associates
San Diego City Schools
Sarjam Communications, Ltd.
Schreiber Translations, Inc.
Seattle/King County Convention & Visitors Bureau
SH3, Inc.
Simultrans, L.L.C.
Southwest Washington Medical Center
Spacelabs Medical
Spectrum Multilanguage Communications
Statistica, Inc.
Summer Institute of Linguistics - Translation Dept.
Suzuki Myers & Associates, Ltd.
Sykes Enterprises, Inc.
TCL & E (Training Consultants for Learnings & Enhancement)
Techlingua, Inc.
Techno-graphics & Translations, Inc.
Terra Pacific Writing Corporation
Thammasat University
TIICO-Translating Interpreting Int'l Co.
The Toin Corporation
Toward, Inc.
Traductions Des Rives, Inc.
Trans Pacific Communications
Transact
Transemantics, Inc.
Translating Concepts
Translation Aces, Inc.
Translation Company of America, Inc.
Translation News

Translex International
Translingua, Inc.
Transperfect
Transtek Associates, inc.
Tru Lingua Language Systems, Inc.
University Language Center, Inc.
The University of Findlay
University of Hawaii
University of Nebraska at Kearney
University of Washington - Language Learning Center
University of Washington Medical Center
Van Oberbeek Translations
Vision Graphics International, Inc.
Vocalesis Interpreting & Translating Services
Wang Laboratories, Inc.
Western Michigan University
William L. Gray Enterprises, Inc.
Word Communication International
Word Design, Inc.
The Wordmill
Wordnet, Inc.
World Bank
World Cultures Institute, Inc.
ZML Software Systems, Inc.
ZMS Communications, Inc.

American Translators Association Officers and Board of Directors, 1994

Edith Losa, President
Anne Cordero, Secretary

Peter Krawutschke, President-Elect
Seth A. Reames, Treasurer

William I. Bertsche, Bonnie Carson, Kurt Gingold, Nicholas Hartmann, Muriel Jerome-O'Keeffe, Jane E. Maier, Manouche Ragsdale, Charles M. Stacy, Jane M. Zorrilla

Recipients of the Alexander Gode Medal

1964 Alexander Gode (deceased)
1965 Kurt Gingold
1966 Richard & Clara Winston (deceased)
1967 The National Translation Center (defunct)
1968 Pierre-François Caillé (deceased)
1969 Henry Fischbach
1970 Carl V. Bertsche (deceased)
1971 Lewis Bertrand (deceased)
1972 Lewis Galantière (deceased)
1973 Jean-Paul Vinay
1974 Eliot F. Beach
1975 Frederick Ungar (deceased)
1976 No award
1977 Eugene A. Nida
1978 Royal L. Tinsley, Jr.
1979 No award

1980 Gregory Rabassa
1981 Georgetown University, Monterey Institute of International Studies, State University of New York at Binghamton
1982 No award
1983 Françoise Cestac
1984 Charles M. Stern (deceased)
1985 Ludmilla Callaham (deceased) and Richard Ernst
1986 William I. Bertsche
1987 Patricia E. Newman
1988 Marilyn Gaddis Rose
1989 No award
1990 Ben Teague
1991 No award
1992 Deanna L. Hammond
1993 Karl Kummer